Joel's Prophecy

Past and Future

Michael Penny

ISBN: 978-1-78364-438-4

The Open Bible Trust
Fordland Mount, Upper Basildon,
Reading, RG8 8LU, UK.

www.obr.org.uk

Contents

Reviews of the first edition

This is a verse by verse exposition of the book of Joel, followed by a study of its application in Acts chapter 2. In his usual racy style, the author rejects the interpretation commonly held by Pentecostals and charismatics, arguing that a correct understanding can only be gained by carefully considering the original text. Helpful maps, diagrams and indexes make this book excellent value for money.
(Reviewed in *The Methodist Recorder,* UK)

Another book from the fluent pen of Michael Penny. This is a verse by verse exposition of Joel followed by a study of its application in the New Testament.
(Reviewed in *A Bookstalls Newsletter*, UK)

Preface

Can any passage of Scripture have as many interpretations attributed to it as does Acts Chapter 2? So much is read into those verses by some and yet so much is left out by others. The varying interpretations have been the cause of one of the biggest rifts in Christendom and yet, so few have taken the trouble of studying the prophet whose message seems to be at the centre of the confusion. Many know the five verses quoted by Peter on the Day of Pentecost but what was the context of those words? What did Peter understand by them? What did Joel mean by them? What was the whole of Joel's message? When we can appreciate that, then we may start to comprehend what Peter meant in Acts Chapter 2.

Another reason for such diversity of opinion over these important verses is that many have argued from *experience* to *doctrine.* Thus the passage has been "made to fit" what has happened in the lives of a wide variety of people. The experiences have not been identical and so that passage of Scripture gets pulled in various directions. It is our contention that *doctrine* should be based on the Bible and our *experiences* must then be interpreted in the light of what the Bible states. This may mean modifying or even rejecting some of our experiences but, if Peter could say that the Scriptures were a "more sure word of prophecy" than the transfiguration he experienced, then we would do well to follow him, (2 Peter 1:16-19).

Michael Penny

1. Background

Introduction

In these writings we shall assume that the reader has no knowledge of Joel's prophecy and little, if any, knowledge of much of the Old Testament. Thus we crave the patience of our more knowledgeable readers but in this day and age, when so few are well-acquainted with God's Word, this must be the right approach.

One may ask why deal with the prophecy of Joel? Is it a book of such great importance for the new Christian? Are there not other, more important, parts of the Bible that deserve people's time and attention? Answers to these questions may vary but Peter's quotation from Joel on the Day of Pentecost (Acts 2:17-21) has thrown this prophecy into the limelight. Sadly, however, few know the context of Peter's quotation and this book is an endeavour to look at Joel's prophecy as a whole and in its Old Testament setting. When we have done that then we will look at Peter's usage of the prophecy.

Where is Joel's prophecy?

Towards the end of the Old Testament is a group of relatively small books called the Minor Prophets: these start with Hosea and then comes Joel, Amos, Obadiah ... and so on till we get to the last book of the Old Testament, Malachi. In all, there are twelve Minor Prophets and they make interesting reading. However, before studying Joel we need to read it and this will not take long. There are only 73 verses and these are split into three chapters and to read the whole book takes less than ten minutes.

Most of the book of Joel is written in Hebrew poetry and if you have read the King James Version (*KJV*) or the Revised Version (*RV*) or J.N. Darby's translation (*JND*) this will have escaped you for these do not attempt to put the English into any type of poetry or verse form.

However The Revised Standard Version (*RSV*), Moffatt, the New English Bible (*NEB*) and the New International Version (*NIV*) do their best to translate the Hebrew poetry into some equivalent English form.

It is probably a good idea to read Joel's prophecy in two different translations and although we will be quoting from other translations, we shall quote mainly from the *King James Version* and the *New International Version*.

When you first read this prophecy the meaning of some of the verses will be obvious — others will be perplexing. In certain cases it is clear that the words should be taken literally and in others figuratively but in some cases ... it is hard to tell. However before *studying* any book of the Bible it is a good idea to *read* it through, if possible, two or three times. Thus before proceeding please read Joel's prophecy through two or three times. This will take about twenty to thirty minutes.

Who was Joel?

Before starting on a detailed study of the book it may be useful to know something about the person God inspired to write it. Also it may be useful to know where he wrote it, when he wrote and what was the situation (political, economic, sociological as well as religious) at the time of writing. Also it may help to know why God inspired the book to be written. If any of these questions (Who? When? Where? What? Why?)[1] are important or if any are essential to our understanding of the book, then the relevant details will be abundantly clear. However, if any are of no consequence to the interpretation then the details of such will be lacking.

Who was Joel? Nothing is known of him other than what is contained in

---

[1] The principle of asking these five questions was set out by Miles Coverdale in the preface to the first *printed* English Bible. They also form the basis of Michael Penny's book *Approaching the Bible* (published by the Open Bible Trust) which was written to help people study for themselves.

this prophecy. Some think he might have been a priest as he was very concerned about the priests and the offerings in the Temple – see 'Where was Joel' in two pages time. However, in Joel 1:13 the expression "ye priests" (*KJV*), which some see as him distancing himself from the priests, implies he is not one of them. All we know is that he is the son of Pethuel, Joel 1:1, and we know nothing more about this Pethuel either. In fact Pethuel is a very unusual name and occurs nowhere else in the Bible. The Greek translation of the Old Testament, the Septuagint (*LXX*), puts the name as Bethuel.

However, Joel was relatively a common name; there are twelve different Joels in the Old Testament, and "son of Pethuel" is added to the name to distinguish this Joel from any other. Thus the people of his day would know which Joel it was who had given out this "word of the Lord" but it is not important for us to know. For us to understand what is written we need know nothing about the inspired writer but we have been given his name.

To describe fully the great God Who surpasses our comprehension is impossible. However in an attempt to let us have a glimpse of His magnificence He uses different names, titles and descriptions of Himself. Two of the most common in the Old Testament are *Elohim* and *Jehovah*.

Elohim is the word used for God with respect to creation and *Jehovah* is the word used for God with respect to the covenants He made with His people. *Elohim* is the great, all powerful God of creation and *Jehovah* is the same great, all powerful Creator in covenant relation with mankind, His creatures. Now *El*, the almighty God, is a contraction of *Elohim*, and *Jah* is a contraction of *Jehovah* and is used to depict *Jehovah* with respect to the special covenant of salvation.

Thus the name 'Joel' is a mixture of these two names of God and means "Jehovah is God". Another interesting name is 'Elijah' which has these two names in reverse order and means "My God is Jehovah". Two very appropriate names for two of God's prophets.

When was the Prophecy of Joel written?

Of the twelve Minor Prophets six are dated and six are not dated. Joel's prophecy is undated but a clue to the date can be obtained by internal evidence, that is noting what is contained in the book and comparing it with what is written elsewhere in the Old Testament. However this can never be accurate and different opinions are possible.

Joel's prophecy may be undated because *when* the prophecy was written, and the situation *at that* time, may not have been important. It may be undated because the burden of the book is in the future, the time of the end, "the Day of the Lord". Thus the prophecy took the people of Joel's day out of their present time and situation, and focused their minds on future events.

We could go into a lot of detail dealing with the different interpretations of the internal evidence for the dating of the book but this does not seem profitable at this point. It is perhaps worth noting that there are three main ideas:

(1) Some think it was written very early either:
a) in the days of Athaliah's usurpation (787-782 B.C.), or
b) in the days of King Jehoash (781-744 B.C.), or
c) in the days of King Uzziah (701-649 B.C.).
(2) Some think it was written in the last days of the kingdom of Judah, just before the Temple was destroyed and the nation taken to Babylon (488-477 B.C.).
(3) Some think it was written in the days after the nation returned to the land following the Babylonian captivity (444-345 B.C., probably about 400 B.C.).

If the dating was important it would have been recorded for us (see Hosea 1:1 and Amos 1:1) but as it was not, we will say no more at this point. The above just demonstrates that when there is not clear guidance from God men soon disagree!

With respect to the above dates we have followed the chronology given by Dr. E.W. Bullinger in *The Companion Bible*. The dating of the kings and the prophets is not easy and scholars do disagree but this is not the subject before us now.[2]

Where was Joel?

The people of Israel were a united nation under their first three kings for most of the 120 years. Saul, David and Solomon each reigned for 40 years but at Solomon's death the nation split in two. The northern kingdom of ten tribes was called Israel and its capital was .Samaria. The southern kingdom of two tribes (Judah and Benjamin) was called Judah and Jerusalem was its capital. From chapter 3 and verses 1, 6, 8, 18, 19, 20 we are left in no doubt that Joel was concerned with Judah and, from 2:32 and 3:1, 6, 16, 17, 20, Jerusalem. In chapter 1 verses 9 and 13, and in chapter 2 verse 17 the priesthood is indicated and in 1:9, 13 and 2:14 the offerings are mentioned. Thus Joel seems to be right in the centre of things, dealing with events at the Temple of Jerusalem, the capital of Judah.

Although Israel was originally the name of the northern kingdom only, the term came to be used of both parts. Similarly, the expression "the people of Israel" could refer to either those of the northern kingdom or both kingdoms and the context must decide the precise meaning. Joel 3:1,6,20 speaks of "Judah and Jerusalem" 3:8,18,19 refers to "Judah"; 2:32 and 3:16,17 focuses on "Jerusalem"; but 3:2,16 uses the expression the "people of Israel" and 2:27 has just "Israel". Thus we may infer that Joel's prophecy concerns both parts of the house if Israel, all Twelve Tribes.

What was the situation?

Being unable to give an exact date of writing means we are unable to give, with certainty, the exact situation but we will at this stage narrow

---

[2] For alternative dating see *Biblical Chronology* by Peter John-Charles, and *The Believer's Guide to Bible Chronology* by Charles Ozanne, both available from The Open Bible Trust; www.obt.org.uk furnishes more details of these two books.

Joel's Prophecy: Past and Future

the dating down.

We feel that an early dating is unlikely to be correct as neither Israel nor Judah were in captivity or even under the threat of captivity. If there was no such threat, then the words of Joel 3:1 would have been inappropriate. If Joel completed his prophecy in those early days then "there is no historical background for Joel's burning words concerning Judah and the great 'Day of the Lord'" (*The Companion Bible,* page 1224).

Two possible datings are now left — either just before Judah was taken into captivity by Nebuchadnezzar or after their return from that captivity. Bearing in mind the great plea to "repent" (Joel 1:13-20; 2:12-17) the former of these seems the most probable. It has been suggested that the image for Joel's prophecy was an exceptionally severe plague of locusts, possibly preceded by a drought, and followed by a bush fire in the days just prior to Judah being taken into captivity. The case for this possibility will be strengthened when we look at the book in detail. However, whatever different views we may hold, we will all agree that this prophecy was given to the people of Judah when they were low; drought, locusts and fire had destroyed their crops and the thought of captivity, either pending or having just ended, was in their mind.

Why was it written?

The prophet Hosea was sent to *guilty* Israel, the northern kingdom. The prophet Joel was sent to Judah, the *guilty* southern kingdom, and his words relate to the end of the kingdom of Judah and impending captivity. It contains several calls for the nation to change their ways (1:13-14 and 2:12-17) and exhorts them to turn to the Lord. If they would do this then God would not only be merciful (2:13-14) but He would also bestow upon them gifts and give them signs (2:18-32). He would also judge the nations that pursue and embattle them (3:12). Thus Joel's prophecy was given to encourage Judah to repent of their wicked ways and so avoid an imminent enemy.

If we are correct in placing this book in the years just prior to the Babylonian captivity (488-477 B.C.) then the books of Kings and

Chronicles will be a help. These are the "history" books of the Old Testament and 2 Kings 24 and 25 and 2 Chronicles 36 cover the closing years of the nation of Judah and if you read these three chapters you will see that the kingdom of Judah was displeasing the Lord and the kings of Judah did "that which was evil" in the sight of the Lord. No doubt many were caught up in this evil, especially the leaders of Judah, and Joel was sent to call them to repent and to change their ways, saying that if they did so and turned to the Lord, He would be merciful and bestow great blessings upon them. This is the burden of Joel's prophecy. Did the people respond? Sadly history tells us that they did not and judgment resulted in a period of captivity in Babylon.

Why didn't the people respond? Didn't Joel put the case strongly enough or thoroughly enough? Was his message not clear enough? Didn't he convince them that his message was from the Lord? Well, we will find out the answers to these later but before proceeding, read Joel again and the following outline of Joel's Prophecy may be of help.

Joel's Prophecy: Past and Future

```
1:1    "The Word of the Lord"
    1:2,3        Call to hear
    1:4-13       Judgments   inflicted on Judah
                 1:4-7       New wine cut off
                 1:8-13      Harvest spoilt
    1:14-2:17 Call to repent
                 1:14-2:14   Judah a desolation
                 2:15-17     The gathering of Judah
    2:18-3:21 Judgments   removed from Judah
                 2:18        The Lord will be jealous
                 2:19        The Lord will answer
                 2:20        I will remove
                 2:21-27     I will restore
                 2:28-29     I will pour out My Spirit
                 2:30-32     I will show wonders
                 3:1         I will restore
                 3:2         I will gather the nations
                 3:2-8       1 will plead
                 3:9-17      The Gentile harvest
                 3:18        New wine restored
                 3:19-21     Egypt and Sodom a desolation
3:21    "The Lord dwells in Zion".
```

On Page 1224 of *The Companion Bible* Dr. E.W. Bullinger gives his structure for this book:

		1:1 The Title
A	1:2,3	Call to hear
B	1:4-13	Judgments. Inflicted
A	1:14-2:17	Call to repent
B	2:18-3:21	Judgments. Removed.

On page 262 of volume 25 of *The Berean Expositor* Mr C.H. Welch suggests that the following may be of help to the reader:

A a	1:7	New wine cut off
b	1:8-13	Israel's harvest spoiled
B	1:14-2:14	Israel a desolation
C	2:15-20	The gathering of Israel
D	2:21-3:1	I will restore
C	3:2	The gathering of nations
D	3:2-8	I will plead
A b	3:9-17	Gentile harvest
a	3:18	New wine restored
B	3:19-21	Egypt and Edom a desolation

The chapter divisions in our Bibles, and indeed the verses, were put in by man and they make study and reference much, much easier. However there were no such divisions in the original, inspired writings and there are places where the break is inappropriate, spoiling the flow of the message. In order to compare similar sentiments and to contrast differing ones, the use of structures is an aid — breaking down and cutting across the rigidity of chapters and verses. Different writers often present different structures, and we will produce a detailed one at the end of our study of Joel, but in the meantime the reader may care to note for himself passages which repeat and emphasize similar thoughts and ideas and those which directly contrast with one another.

Whichever of the above two structures we choose to follow we see that there is a change at the end of verse 13. Thus in this study it would seem to be appropriate to consider the first thirteen verses of the opening chapter of Joel's prophecy.

2. Joel 1:1-13

Joel 1:1: The Word of the Lord (Jehovah) that came to Joel the son of Pethuel.

This opening verse shows that what Joel is going to write is not his word but the Lord's. Joel can be described as one of those holy men of God who "spoke from God as they were carried along by the Holy Spirit." (2 Peter 1:21). This then fixes our attitude. What we have before us is a message from the Lord and so, we must treat it as such. Being respectful and studious, and exercising humility over those parts which we cannot understand, will be far more profitable than dismissing some of what follows as "impossible" or "fantastic" or .. .

The Hebrew for "word", in Joel 1:1, is *dabar* and does not necessarily mean a spoken word. It can mean "matter" or "subject" in a more general sense. Thus although nearly all translations open with the expression "The word of the Lord", Moffatt has "The message of the Eternal" (Moffatt always uses 'Eternal' to translate *Jehovah)*. Here Joel stresses the source of his message, his revelation, is not himself but the Lord and this is reinforced in Joel 2:12 with "saith the Lord" (*KJV*); "declares the Lord" (*NIV*).

"The word of the Lord" is also the opening of other prophecies. See, for example, the first verses of Hosea, Micah and Zephaniah. Their prophecies, too, were also from the Lord and expressions like "says the Lord" or "declares the Lord" must occur well over four hundred times throughout the Old Testament, indicating and emphasizing, time and time again, that what is contained therein is "The word of the Lord", "The message of the Eternal".

Joel 1:2-3: Hear this, you elders; listen, all who live in the land. Has anything like this ever happened in your days or in the days of your forefathers? Tell it to your children, and let your children tell it to their children, and their children to the next generation.

Joel, having received a revelation from the Lord, promptly tells others about it but he does not stop there. He encourages and exhorts them to tell their children the message. But not only that, he also urges them to ensure that their children will tell their children and that they, in their turn, will tell their children. The importance of the message is emphasized by telling the old to ensure that, as well as their children and grandchildren knowing it, their great grandchildren must hear it also.

With an appeal to the old men and the past, "Has such a thing happened in your days, or in the days of your fathers?" (*RSV*), Joel emphasizes the seriousness of the events. This swarm of locusts, and its devastating effect, may have brought into the minds of the inhabitants of Judah and Jerusalem the words of Exodus 10:3-15. Then the land of Egypt had been infested by such a plague of locusts because Pharaoh had not allowed Moses and the people to go and worship the Lord. Pharaoh was sinning against the Lord, disobeying His commands and so ... judgment. Was this plague, the one which preceded this message of Joel, the result of the people of Judah sinning against and disobeying the Lord? Certainly if it was written in the days just prior to the Babylonian exile then various verses in 2 Kings 24 and 25 and 2 Chronicles 36 are appropriate, recording that the kings "did evil in the sight of the Lord".

The word for 'old men' (v 2, *KJV*) is *zaqen*, which is translated 'elders' in 1:14 and 2:16; and translated 'elders' in all three verses of the *NIV*. Apparently either is a possible translation but here, in verses 2 and 3, Joel is encouraging the people to look as far into the future as they can and as far back into the past as is possible. Thus "old men", rather than "elders", may be more appropriate. However, the majority of the "elders" would be "old men" so perhaps we are splitting hairs.

Joel 1:4-13: Judgments inflicted.

Joel 1:4: What the locust swarm has left the great locusts have eaten; what the great locusts have left the young locusts have eaten; what the young locusts have left other locusts have eaten.

Joel, having made the claim that his message is from the Lord and having exhorted his people to listen, now launches into that message. He opens with a very short but very sharp punch-line which would make those who heard sit up. The English of Joel 1:4, in both the *NIV* and the *KJV,* is very graphic but in the Hebrew there are but twelve words and *The Companion Bible* suggests the following translation of the opening of Joel's message:

> Gnawer's remnant, Swarmer eats:
> Swarmer's remnant, Devourer eats:
> Devourer's remnant, Consumer eats.

Such terrible and overwhelming destruction would certainly gain the attention of any listener and reader but how difficult it is to translate such expressions into easily understood English. The KJV has:

> That which the palmerworm hath left
>   hath the locust eaten:
>   and that which the locust hast left
>   hath the cankerworm eaten;
> and that which the cankerworm has left
>   hath the caterpillar eaten.

As there are over ninety types of locust, and as there are ten different Hebrew words used for locust, the exact translation / interpretation of this verse is difficult. *The Companion Bible* points out that palmer-worm is *gazam,* the gnawer, and is the first of four different stages of the locust. In England we might describe this as the hairy caterpillar. Next, Joel 1:4, is locust — *arbeh';* the swarmer. This is the imago or adult stage. Canker worm is *yelek,* the devourer, and caterpillar is *hasil,* the consumer and possibly the larva stage.

JND has the same translation as the *KJV* but adds notes: "probably different species of locusts or different stages in growth, as 'grub', 'creeper', 'feeder'." He goes on to suggest that the cankerworm, literally "the feeder", may be a locust in the stage just before it arrives in the perfect, imago stage and in which it devours much vegetation.

Thankfully not living in a land affected by these creatures, one is at a loss to unravel the details of this verse but so too, or so it appears, are the translators of the *NIV*:

> What the locust swarm has left
> 　　the great locusts have eaten:
> What the great locusts have left
> 　　the young locusts have eaten;
> What the young locusts have left
> 　　other locusts have eaten.

The translators, however, add a note saying "the precise meaning of the four Hebrew words used here for locusts is uncertain", but what is certain is that *everything* has been eaten! There is nothing left! There is terrible devastation. That is Joel's point and although we might have problems fully appreciating the finer details of this verse we can most surely "get the message". In poetic style, Joel brings home the fact. The plague of locusts has destroyed everything!

What the cutting locust left, the swarming locust has eaten. What the swarming locust left, the hopping locust has eaten, What the hopping locust left, the destroying locust has eaten. (*RSV*)	What the lopping locust left, the swarming locust ate. What the swarming locust left, the leaping locust ate, and what the leaping locust left, the devouring locust ate" (*Moffatt*)

Moffatt, certainly, with alliteration of "lopping locust left" and "leaping locust left" perhaps comes nearest to a poetic representation of this verse.

We have spent some time on this verse because Joel reveals the main purpose of his prophecy through a double reference to locusts. The first, in Joel 1:4, would cause further depression to his already dejected listeners. They already knew the consequences of the plague and would not welcome being reminded. His next reference, however, should gladden their hearts and lift the clouds of despondency:

"I will repay you for the years the locusts have eaten - the great locust and the young locust, the other locusts and the locust swarm - my great army that I sent among you. You will have plenty to eat, until you are full, and you will praise the name of the LORD your God, who has worked wonders for you; never again will my people be shamed." (Joel 2:25-26)

Thus the theme of Joel, as it is in many of the other prophets, is the threat of impending judgment, but its climax, like the other prophets, is the restoration of the peoples of Israel and Judah into one kingdom under the Kingship of the Lord.

Joel 1:5-13

Having dealt with the cause of the destruction in verse 4, Joel now proceeds to describe that destruction, picking out several particular items. The structure of this section enables us to highlight these.

1:5a	PEOPLE	Call to wake up and wail
1:5b-7	REASON	Vine laid waste and fig tree ruined
1:8	LAND	Call to mourn
1:9,10	REASON	Offerings are cut off
1:11a	PEOPLE	Call to be despair and wail
1:11b,12	REASON	Harvest perished and trees withered
1:13a	PRIESTS	Call to mourn
1:13b	REASON	Offerings withheld.

Joel 1:5: Wake up, you drunkards, and weep! Wail, all you drinkers of wine; wail because of the new wine, for it has been snatched from your lips

The drunkards are told to awake and "all you drinkers of wine" are told to howl. In those days "all you drinkers of wine" would include nearly everyone — the only general exception being those who chose to be Nazarites (Numbers 6:2-21). Apart from fresh milk there was little else to drink. The water could not be relied upon to be free of infection and it could not be stored for long. The fermentation process, necessary for the production of wine, does allow the product to be stored for quite some time afterwards. The apparent conflict between "new wine" (*NIV*, *KJV*) and "sweet wine" (*RSV*) is only apparent. New wine would always be sweet for the longer the fermentation lasts, the less sweet the wine and the greater its alcoholic content. Thus sweet, low alcoholic wines would be popular and one can be sure that Joel is addressing practically the whole of the population. Even some who took the Nazarite vow, which involved abstention from wine, did not always keep it; see Amos 2:11,12. So we can safely say that this somewhat derisory description ...

> Wake up you tipplers and weep, wail,
> every swiller of wine (Moffatt) ...

embraces practically the whole of Judah. Such an expression is apt for a people exhorted to repent of their wrong and turn again to God. Not only that, these people are told to wake up and wail because "the new wine ... has been snatched from your lips", "cut off from your mouth" (*KJV*). This would indicate that the plague had arrived just before the grape harvest. What a bitter blow! Just when they were thinking of picking the grapes ... destruction!

Joel 1:6: A nation has invaded my land, powerful and without number; it has the teeth of a lion, the fangs of a lioness.

Next the people are told to wake up and wail because a nation has come upon God's land — note the 'my' land. The word for nation is *goy* and here it seems that the locusts are called a nation just as ants are called a "people" in Proverbs 30:25. However some assert that this word *goy*, which is translated 'nation' or 'Gentiles', cannot refer to locusts. They interpret the four descriptions of Joel 1:4 as the four Gentile super powers which were to rule over this land until our Lord Jesus Christ's time on earth, and beyond. Daniel's interpretation of Nebuchadnezzar's dream (Daniel 2:27-45), and other parts of Daniel, may well refer to these nations of Babylon, Persia, Greece and Rome, but to read these into Joel 1:4 is perhaps forcing a prophetic and allegorical interpretation onto a past and literal event.

Verse 7 goes on to say that this 'nation' has "laid waste my vines" and "ruined my fig trees". It has "stripped off the bark", all indicating a 'nation' of locusts, rather than a 'nation' of Gentiles. Certainly this opening chapter of Joel is a very 'agricultural' section and the straight-forward interpretation of verses 4-7 allows them to stay in their obvious context of natural events of that day.

Again some may say that the description given in this verse is not fitting for locusts but "teeth of a lion" and "fangs of a lioness" (*NIV*) are most appropriate for creatures that are so destructive. R.A. Cole mentions an Arab saying which credits the locust with the "chest of a lion", maybe because of its appearance but possibly because of its destructiveness. Thus although Joel is a prophecy which undoubtedly deals with apocalyptic and allegorical symbols in its later passages, we are perhaps wiser in not reading such into the opening verses.

Joel 1:7: It has laid waste my vines and ruined my fig trees. It has stripped off their bark and thrown it away, leaving their branches white.

Verses 6 and 7 are vivid, poetic descriptions of the ravaging of a swarm of locusts. Thus there is much reason for the people to wail and howl. When the creatures have eaten all the leaves then they attack the bark. Everything that the people of Judah relied upon for sustenance ... gone! The vine was laid waste and the fig trees ruined, stripped of its bark. The corn or grain was destroyed and the olive tree mutilated and unable to produce its oil (verse 10). Throughout the whole of this section again note the Lord referring to 'my' land, 'my' vine, 'my' fig tree. He is the Creator of all things (John 1:3) and as such all belong to Him.

Joel 1:8: Mourn like a virgin in sackcloth grieving for the husband of her youth.

In the third line of the structure for Joel 1:5-13 there is the call for the 'land to lament'. This, according to *The Companion Bible*, is because the word for 'lament' in verse 8 is feminine and agrees with and qualifies the word for 'land' in verse 6. How that land is to lament! Think of the havoc these creatures have wreaked upon it. It was terrible and certainly it would be hard for Joel to find a stronger figure to describe this lamentation than the one he has used. "A virgin girded with sackcloth" (*KJV*) is perhaps the supreme symbol of grief depicting, as it does, a girl whose fiancé has been killed just before their wedding. In Joel's day, in the land of Judah, an engagement was as binding as a wedding and this was still the case during the New Testament times, as we see from Joseph's predicament over Mary (Matthew 1:18,19). Thus for a young girl to lose her fiancé ... well, I am sure we can all appreciate the sadness of that situation. It was to guard against such terrible grief as this that the Lord, through Moses and the Law, did not allow engaged men to serve in the military (see Deuteronomy 20:7 and 24:5).

Joel 1:9: Grain offerings and drink offerings are cut off from the house of the LORD. The priests are in mourning, those who minister before the LORD.

The land is called to lament because it has been unable to yield the "grain offering" and the "drink offering". The "meat offering" (*KJV*) is better called the 'meal' offering or 'grain' offering for it does not require blood, the killing of an animal. Animal sacrifices were to secure admittance into God's presence but the grain offering was a gift to secure favour. It is fully described in Leviticus 2 which mentions fine flour and oil as the main ingredients but green ears of corn could be used. Bearing in mind Joel 1:10 (the grain is destroyed) we see that such offerings were now impossible.

The drink offering is mentioned in conjunction with the grain offering in Leviticus 23:13, and in Exodus 29:40 it is linked with the sacrifice of the lamb. Numbers 15:3-10 connects it with several different offerings. Thus it was quite important.

In Hebrew the drink offering is *nesek* which is derived from *nasak* which means to pour out and this, literally, was what was done with the drink offering. It was poured out onto a stone pillar (Genesis 35:14). Again, bearing in mind that this drink offering was either wine or a mixture of wine and oil and, noting that both of these ingredients had been destroyed by the locusts (Joel 1:7), we see that it was impossible for the people to offer these sacrifices. At such times of drought and plague the people could easily have offered the animal sacrifices. At such times, when there was no vegetation to feed the flocks, they would probably have gladly offered them, but often the animal sacrifices needed to be accompanied by the grain and drink offerings, and that was now impossible (Exodus 29:40,41).

The priests, the Lord's ministers, are told to mourn and when one appreciates fully their connection with the offerings then the absence of such would cause them great concern. Those who claim that the expression "The Lord's ministers" indicates that Joel was written after the Babylonian exile because it is a "late" expression, fail to note that similar expressions occur elsewhere in the books known to have been written before the exile (e.g. Jeremiah 33:21). Also the sentiments of ministering go back much earlier and are found in such passages as Exodus 30:20 and Numbers 3:6.

Joel 1:10: The fields are ruined, the ground is dried up; the grain is destroyed, the new wine is dried up, the oil fails.

The priests mourn and the land laments and the ground groans because of the absence of the offerings. The land was unable to provide the oil and flour and corn but its predicament was worse than that. The land "mourns" as the *NIV* footnote and *KJV* put it.

The word 'ground' in verse 10 is *adamah* and is elsewhere translated 'soil' or 'land'. It is not the word translated 'land' in verses 2, 6 and 14 which is *erets*, meaning land or country.

> The fields are ruined,
>> the ground is dried up;
>>> the grain is destroyed,
>>>> the new wine is dried up,
>>>>> the oil fails.

Such is the lament of the land!

Joel 1:11-12: Despair, you farmers, wail, you vine growers; grieve for the wheat and the barley, because the harvest of the field is destroyed. The vine is dried up and the fig tree is withered; the pomegranate, the palm and the apple tree - all the trees of the field - are dried up. Surely the joy of mankind is withered away.

Now certain groups of people are told to despair, wail and grieve. Bearing in mind this was an agricultural community, those described in this verse would be most of the population.

"Be ye ashamed, O ye husbandmen" (*KJV*) is not the clearest rendering.

> Despair you farmers — wail, you vine growers. (*NIV*)
> The farmer is downcast — the vinedresser wails. (Moffatt)

These are perhaps better. Certainly the farmers have much to despair about, the vine growers much to wail about. The rest of verse 11 and verse 12 give the sad story.

Verses 10 to 12 are indeed serious and to ensure that the listener's and reader's attention is fully grasped they are full of assonance, that is the words used have a similar sound or they may rhyme. In this passage there is the repetition of words similar in sound but different in meaning. This can be termed paronomasia.

The opening words of verse 10 are, in English, "The fields are ruined". In Hebrew 'field' is *sadeh* and 'wasted' is *shadad;* so we get the assonance *sadeh shadad.* Thus our readers may get the picture and will, at the same time, appreciate the impossibility of translating such a passage and keeping that figure of speech. However Moffat makes moving reading:

The fields are blasted the land woebegone,
> for the corn is wasted,
>> the wine crop fails,
>>> the fresh oil dries up.
The farmer is downcast, the vine-dresser wails,
> for the wheat and the barley,
>> the harvest of the field is ruined,
> the vines are languishing,
>> the fig trees wither,
> pomegranate, palm and apple,
>> every tree of the field is a-drooping,
and joy fades from men.

In these verses we see why the offering cannot be brought to the priests and the conclusion of verse 12 is indeed touching — "joy fades from men".

Joel 1:13: Put on sackcloth, O priests, and mourn; wail, you who minister before the altar. Come, spend the night in sackcloth, you who minister before my God; for the grain offerings and drink offerings are withheld from the house of your God.

It is now the priest's turn and they are called to lament. These ministers of the altar (Exodus 30:20) are called to howl. These ministers of God are called to lie in sackcloth all night, maybe to exemplify David in 2 Samuel 12:16, but sackcloth was a standard symbol of mourning (Joel 1:8).

Here the priests are told to mourn and wail because they can no longer perform their duties. They can no longer serve the Lord in the way He had instructed. They cannot accept the people's offerings to God because there are no offerings; there is nothing to offer. The land gives the offerings to the people, and the priests accept them from the people. Thus, in the structure, the land's call to mourn and the priest's call to mourn are paralleled. They are interlinked. Both priests and land lament, because there are no offerings.

With this sorry state of affairs we finish this section. It has been a long one and a somewhat depressing one but throughout it all one can sense that the Lord is in control. It is *His* land that is called to lament. It is *His* vine which is laid waste, *His* fig tree laid bare and the offerings which *He* instituted have been cut off but …

> Who knows? He [the LORD] may turn and have pity and leave behind a blessing - grain offerings and drink offerings for the LORD your God. (Joel 2:14)

In verse 13 the priests are called to put on sackcloth and mourn, symbols of repentance. We now turn to the section which starts with the call for all who live in the land to repent.

3. Joel 1:14 - 2:11

Joel 1:14-3:21 can come under the heading "call to repent". Its structure is as follows:

1:14	Call to fast
1:15	Reason
1:16-20	Consequences
2:1a	**People**: Call to blow the trumpet
2:1b	Reason
2:2-11	Consequences
2:12-13a	Call to fast
2:13b	Reason
2:14	Consequences
2:15-17a	**Priests:** Call to blow the trumpet
2:17b	Reason
2:18-3:21	Consequences

In this chapter we shall look at the first half of this structure; that is Joel 1:14 - 2:11.

Joel 1:14: Declare a holy fast; call a sacred assembly. Summon the elders and all who live in the land to the house of the LORD your God, and cry out to the LORD.

The call by Joel for a solemn, sacred assembly should remind the people of Judah of similar events recorded in the law of Moses (Leviticus 23:36; Num. 29:35; Deuteronomy 16:8). At these, the people were told to do no regular work but to bring sacrifices and so, as the sacrifices were often eaten, there would be food. Here Joel precedes the call for a sacred assembly with the call for a fast, probably because the people were unable to supply certain of the offerings (Joel 1:9,13). However, fasting was associated with the forgiveness of sin, and the Day of Atonement (Leviticus 16:29) was a day of fasting. Thus forgiveness may have been behind the call, for Joel does call the people to repent Joel 1:13-20). Also, bearing in mind that in the past the people had abused the solemn assemblies to such an extent that the Lord had said "it is iniquity, even the solemn meeting" (Isaiah 1:13, *KJV*) and that King Jehu later set up an assembly for the worship of Baal (2 Kings 10:19-21), it may be that Joel wanted to emphasize that such an assembly was of no value unless the heart of the people was penitent

Thus a solemn assembly is called and the people told to fast. All the elders and all the inhabitants of the land are gathered into the house of God and told to "cry unto the Lord". Why?

> … cry out to the LORD.
> Alas for that day!
> For the day of the LORD is near;
> it will come like destruction from the Almighty.

Now however little we may know of this time called "the Day of the Lord", from this verse alone we can see that it is a time to be feared. This Day of the Lord [3] is the theme, from here on, in Joel's prophecy and it occurs in 1:15; 2:1,11,31 and 3:14. From these verses alone we can see how bad it is to be; e.g. the people are told to tremble on this terrible day. We cannot go into the vast detail of this great subject (most of Revelation is about the "Day of the Lord" Revelation 1:10), but suffice it to say that it is characterized by God's judgment upon the earth when He will again break into the world system and vindicate Himself and His people.

The expression first occurs in Isaiah 2:10-19 where a good description is given. In the Day of the Lord man will be abased and the Lord exalted, whereas today self-exaltation by man is common and God has been shut out of the lives of many and almost pushed out of the world He has created. This may be the reason that this age is termed "man's day" - an alternative reading of 1 Corinthians 4:3 — and demonstrates that the time period for the Day of the Lord need not be 24 hours. Still, however

---

[3] For more on this subject see *The Day of the Lord! When?* by Michael Penny, published by the Open Bible Trust.

Joel's Prophecy: Past and Future

bad that day will be for mankind, we should note that God's mercy will always be extended to the humble and repentant sinner (Joel 2:11-13).

Joel 1:16: Has not the food been cut off before our very eyes-- joy and gladness from the house of our God?

Having drawn people's attention to the Day of the Lord, Joel now returns to describe the consequences of this plague of locusts. What he saw left a vivid picture in his mind. This formed a basis for his description of the totally destructive result of the army of people portrayed in chapter 2.

In verse 16 the word "meat" *(KJV)* is translated "food" elsewhere *(NIV, RSV; NIV; JND; Moffatt)*. Not only has the wine been snatched from their lips (1:5) but their food has disappeared from before their eyes. The harvest was nigh, but now there would be no harvest. Thus they could not keep the Feast of Weeks, elsewhere called Pentecost, which was related to the harvest and which was always a time of great rejoicing (Deuteronomy 16:9-12). Similarly the Feast of Tabernacles (Deuteronomy 16:13-15) was a time of immense celebration which took place after the gathering in of the cereal crops and grapes. This must have been in Joel's mind.

Joel 1:17: The seeds are shrivelled beneath the clods. The storehouses are in ruins, the granaries have been broken down, for the grain has dried up.

It is hard to see in verse 17 why the seeds should be "rotten" *(KJV)*. The *RSV* and the *NIV* have "shrivels" and "shrivelled" respectively and that does seem more appropriate. Seeds may rot in times of excess water but never in a time of drought followed by a locust plague followed by a bush fire (1:19).

> Below the clod crumbles the seed,
> the granaries are standing bare,
> barns are in disrepair,
> for what have we to store up there,
> now that the grain has withered. (Moffatt)

Joel 1:18: How the cattle moan! The herds mill about because they have no pasture; even the flocks of sheep are suffering.

However bad man's plight might be at such a time as this, we must never forget that God is the God of *all* creation and feels for *all* His creatures. Thus Joel is inspired to draw the people's attention to the animals. Moffatt's "The herds of cattle huddle together" and the *NIV*'s "The herds mill about" both paint pictures of the behaviour of these poor creatures and this thought is uppermost in Joel's mind when he cries out to the Lord.

Joel 1:19: To you, O LORD, I call, for fire has devoured the open pastures and flames have burned up all the trees of the field.

Perhaps Joel had in mind the words of the Lord recorded by Asaph in Psalm 50:15:

> Call upon me in the day of trouble;
> I will deliver you, and you will honour me.

This exhortation was to those who:

> Sacrifice thank offerings to GOD,
> Fulfill your vows to the Most High. (Psalm 50:14)

Later Joel is to call the people to turn to their God but in 1:19 he is again concerned with the plight of the animals because "fire has devoured the open pastures" (*NIV*). "Open pastures" is better than "wilderness" (*KJV*) for the latter tends to conjure up, in our minds, poor and somewhat barren land. No! This was the "common pasture" and it had been devoured together with the trees. To see the vegetation ravaged by locusts is bad enough, but to see what remains destroyed by fire is totally despairing and utterly depressing.

Some commentators think that the fire of verse 19 is another description of the plague. Some locusts are a reddish brown and when the swarm moves over the land it moves just like a fire and what remains is bare and barkless — just as if there had been a fire.

Joel 1:20: Even the wild animals pant for you; the streams of water have dried up and fire has devoured the open pastures.

Joel again reminds the people of the animals and draws attention to the fact that the rivers of water had dried up. These "rivers of water", *aphiqim,* were the "water courses" (*Moffatt*) constructed from rocks and pipes and channels and used throughout the land. *Aphiqim* occurs some 15 times in the Old Testament and is translated by various words such as 'channels', 'brooks', 'rivers'. In mentioning the drying up of these courses Joel may have had in mind Psalm 107:33,34:

> He turned rivers into a desert,
> > flowing springs into thirsty ground,
> and fruitful land into a salt waste,
> > because of the wickedness of those who lived there.

We have mentioned before that if Joel was written just prior to the Babylonian exile then such words as the last line above are easily appreciated. Many kings did that which was evil in the sight of the Lord and the implication of Joel's writing is that the calamity which has come upon them is because of the sinfulness of this people. There is now the need to repent.

Joel 2:1-2a: Blow the trumpet in Zion; sound the alarm on my holy hill. Let all who live in the land tremble, for the day of the LORD is coming. It is close at hand - a day of darkness and gloom, a day of clouds and blackness.

This chapter opens with a call to blow the trumpet in Zion, which is another name for Jerusalem, the city of David (2 Samuel 5:6,7). It is accompanied with an order to "sound the alarm on *my* holy hill". Again note the "my", and the "holy hill" is another name for this same city, Zion, Jerusalem (Joel 3:17; Psalm 48:1-2). Some people misunderstand this word 'holy', *qodesh.* It means something or someone separated for or set apart for God. It does not necessarily mean something which is sinless or perfect. In Exodus 3:5 Moses stood on 'holy' ground and it may well have contained thistles and thorns but it was 'holy' because it had been 'set apart' for God.

The blowing of the trumpet and the sounding of the alarm are fully described in Numbers 10:1-9 where the context is preparation for war. The conclusion is "you will be remembered by the LORD your God and rescued from your enemies."

The blowing of the trumpet has also to do with convocations (assemblies) and these are described in Leviticus 23:23-25. At these, the people came together to "offer an offering ... made by fire" and these are described more fully in Exodus 29:18 and its context.

Here, it is unlikely that Joel was ordering the trumpet to be blown to gather the people for the "offering made by fire" because of their inability to supply the grain offering and drink offering which often accompanied such. More probably it was sounded to prepare them for the news of the future and its impending battle. They had just been decimated by the hostile forces of drought, plague and fire; what worse enemy could lie ahead of them? Have they much left to fear? Could anything now cause them greater harm? Well, Joel says:

Let all the inhabitants of the land tremble. (Joel 2:1)

And he gives the reason for such fear:

For the Day of the Lord is coming. It is close at hand. (Joel 2:1)

Joel now moves into the future. Having painted the past in vivid terms and being able to draw analogies from it, he now focuses his attention on events which take place during the "Day of the Lord".

From now on we shall not find these writings very easy to understand and it will be impossible to write with much precision about some of the verses. Viewing fulfilled prophecy in retrospect is relatively easy but to say exactly how unfulfilled prophecy will be accomplished, how all the different prophecies will be drawn together and completed, that is beyond the capabilities of any of us. Let us re-read Joel 2:2-11 again, and meditate upon them, thinking what we can say about them.

Joel 2:2b-11: Like dawn spreading across the mountains a large and mighty army comes, such as never was of old nor ever will be in ages to come. Before them fire devours, behind them a flame blazes. Before them the land is like the garden of Eden, behind them, a desert waste-- nothing escapes them.

They have the appearance of horses; they gallop along like cavalry. With a noise like that of chariots they leap over the mountaintops, like a crackling fire consuming stubble, like a mighty army drawn up for battle. At the sight of them, nations are in anguish; every face turns pale.

They charge like warriors; they scale walls like soldiers. They all march in line, not swerving from their course. They do not jostle each other; each marches straight ahead. They plunge through defenses without breaking ranks. They rush upon the city; they run along the wall. They climb into the houses; like thieves they enter through the windows. Before them the earth shakes, the sky trembles, the sun and moon are darkened, and the stars no longer shine.

The LORD thunders at the head of his army; his forces are beyond number, and mighty are those who obey his command. The day of the LORD is great; it is dreadful. Who can endure it?

Moffatt graphically translates this passage, and on the next page we produce the *NIV* and Moffat in parallel columns for ease of comparison.

NIV	Moffatt
[2] a day of darkness and gloom, a day of clouds and blackness. Like dawn spreading across the mountains a large and mighty army comes, such as never was of old nor ever will be in ages to come.	a dark day in a shroud, a day of fog and cloud here comes a huge host in power, blackening the hills; the like of it never has been, the like of it never shall be, for years upon years to come;

³ Before them fire devours, behind them a flame blazes. Before them the land is like the garden of Eden, behind them, a desert waste— nothing escapes them.	before them fire devouring, behind them flames a blazing: before them the land lies like an Eden paradise, behind them it is a desolate desert for nothing escapes them.
⁴ They have the appearance of horses; they gallop along like cavalry.	They look like horses, they run like war horses,
⁵ With a noise like that of chariots they leap over the mountaintops, like a crackling fire consuming stubble, like a mighty army drawn up for battle.	As chariots rattle, they leap on the hill tops, like flames that crackle, consuming the straw, like a vast army in battle array.
⁶ At the sight of them, nations are in anguish; every face turns pale.	Hearts are in anguish before them, all faces turn pale
⁷ They charge like warriors; they scale walls like soldiers. They all march in line, not swerving from their course.	They charge like warriors, they advance like fighters, each on his own track –
⁸ They do not jostle each other; each marches straight ahead. They plunge through defences without breaking ranks.	no tangling of paths - none pushes his fellow, each follows his own line; they burst through weapons unbroken,
⁹ They rush upon the city; they run along the wall. They climb into the houses; like thieves they enter through the windows.	they rush on the city, run over the walls, climb into houses and enter the windows like thieves.
¹⁰ Before them the earth shakes, the sky trembles, the sun and moon are darkened, and the stars no longer shine.	At their advance the land is quaking, the heavens are shaking, sun and moon are dark, the stars have ceased to shine.
¹¹ The LORD thunders at the head of his army; his forces are beyond number, and mighty are those who obey his command. The day of the LORD is great; it is dreadful. Who can endure it?	And the Eternal thunders in front of His army a mighty host is His, and strong are those who execute His orders. For the Eternal's day is great and awful: who can face it?

Joel's Prophecy: Past and Future

Thank goodness for verse 11! However we interpret the details of verses 2 to 10, it certainly strikes fear into the heart of the reader and one can easily imagine that at this future time, during this Day of the Lord, "every face turns pale" (2:6). So without getting bogged down with the detail, what is described here?

Joel gives us a picture of the greatest army of all time (2:2). It is exceptionally well disciplined (2:7,8) and totally fearless (2:3) and very good (!) at its job (2:7-9). This army is also totally destructive (2:3) and those attacked by it are pale and in anguish (2:6) — but who and what does it attack? Joel 2:9 tells us it is the city; the city where the house of the Lord is, the city in which Joel has gathered all the inhabitants of the land (Joel 1:14). Thus Joel 2:1-10 is describing an attack by a mighty army upon the city of Jerusalem and the Jews who live in it and the surrounding land.

Verse 10 should bring us up with a jolt for it shows us that the power of this army is much greater than can be imagined and, as we shall see, behind this army is the great adversary of God, Satan. Here, in Joel 2:1-10, is described his greatest attempt to wipe the Jew off the face of the earth and so make God break the promises He had made to various people. There are many, many passages to which we could now turn but the following will be sufficient to demonstrate the point.

> This is what the LORD says, he who appoints the sun to shine by day, who decrees the moon and stars to shine by night, who stirs up the sea so that its waves roar - the LORD Almighty is his name:
>
> "Only if these decrees vanish from my sight," declares the LORD, "will the descendants of Israel ever cease to be a nation before me."
>
> This is what the LORD says: "Only if the heavens above can be measured and the foundations of the earth below be searched out will I reject all the descendants of Israel because of all they have done," declares the LORD. (Jeremiah 31:35-37)

However, in Genesis Abraham and his seed were promised a land:

The LORD said to Abram after Lot had parted from him, "Lift up your eyes from where you are and look north and south, east and west. All the land that you see I will give to you and your offspring *forever*. I will make your offspring like the dust of the earth, so that if anyone could count the dust, then your offspring could be counted. Go, walk through the length and breadth of the land, for I am giving it to you." (Genesis 13:14-17)

Thus the seed, the descendants of Israel, and the land are going to endure forever. In the light of this we can see the tremendous challenge in Jeremiah 31:35,36. If the God Who cannot lie (Titus 1:2) and the God Whose gifts and callings are without repentance (Romans 11:29) is made to be a liar and a breaker of promises ... then Satan has victory! Thus in attacking the Jew in his land and in his city, Satan is attempting to wipe the Jew off the face of the earth — so making God break His promise. It seems, also, that he and his army may try and affect the sun, moon and stars in an attempt to make God invoke the promise of Jeremiah 31:35,36. This is the battle of the ages; God v Satan! During the Day of the Lord this battle comes to a head and this future period of time is mainly about that great enemy and his defeat.

When dealing with Satan we must not think of horns, tails and "pitchfork" but should realize that he was, and in some senses still is, the greatest creature of God's creation. He was, so to speak, God's number two — His right hand man, but he wanted more. He was not satisfied. He wanted to be number one, but thankfully that will never be. He has been deposed from his previous position as the accuser of the brethren, being on the right hand of the judge (Revelation 12:10; Psalm 109:6). That position God now occupies Himself in the person of Christ Jesus our Lord (Mark 16:19; Acts 2:33).

We could spend much time in describing Satan but will mention just a few points. He was said to be "the model of perfection, full of wisdom and beauty" and held such titles as the "guardian cherub" (Ezekiel 28:12-19). He is called an "angel of light" and his workers are called "ministers of righteousness" (2 Corinthians 11:14,15); a title indicating their false facade which sadly deceives men. His main desire appears to be to usurp God's position and steal worship from Him. Does he succeed? Well ... we shall wait and see, but although the people of Israel will be no match for his vast army Joel tells us, in 2:11, that there is another army which is mighty beyond number and at the head of that army is the Lord.

Having got the gist and the flow of this passage we will now have a look at one or two details. The first half of Joel 2:2 described the Day of the Lord. Amos 5:18-20 expands this:

> Woe to you who long for the day of the LORD! Why do you long for the day of the LORD? That day will be darkness, not light. It will be as though a man fled from a lion only to meet a bear, as though he entered his house and rested his hand on the wall only to have a snake bite him. Will not the day of the LORD be darkness, not light - pitch-dark, without a ray of brightness?

The second half of Joel 2:2 emphasizes the uniqueness of this still future day and the army with which Satan will pursue the Jew. Revelation 12 is perhaps another description of this battle and related events. Perhaps we are now better able to appreciate the Lord's words in Matthew 24:16 when, referring to this time, He says "Let them which be in Judea flee into the mountains". When there is war, the mountains are safer than the cities.

In Joel 2:8, the word translated 'sword' is *shelakh* and some commentators maintain this is a "late" word and thus Joel must have been written after the Babylonian exile. However the word is found in Job 33:18 and 36:12 and Job is one of the earliest of Old Testament writings. Thus we see no reason to move Joel's prophecy from the days prior to the Babylonian captivity. It also occurs in Song of Songs 4:13 where it is translated "plants".

Some commentators hold the view that the army described in Joel 2:2-10 is the same as that described in Revelation 9:2-11 but a close reading of both passages shows that this cannot be. Whatever is described in Revelation 9 is commanded "not to harm the grass of the earth or any plant or tree" (Revelation 9:4). This directly contradicts Joel 2:3 and what are described in the two passages must be different.

Other commentators claim that the army described in Joel 2:2-10 is the army of the Lord mentioned in verse 11. Knowing how God is to guard and protect this people and feed them as well (Revelation 12:6, 14) during this Day of the Lord, this view seems unlikely. Also, in the light of such passages as Isaiah 51:3 and Ezekiel 36:35, where we are told "this land that was desolate is become like the garden of Eden", we cannot see Joel 2:3 being the work of God's army. Thus we continually come to the conclusion that in Joel 2:2-10 we have a vivid and graphic description of a great attacking force that is to come against Jerusalem and its inhabitants. All seems lost for those people. Their case seems a hopeless one but then ... we are told simply but firmly and clearly (verse 11) that the Lord has His army and His forces are beyond number. The Day of the Lord is great and terrible. Who can endure it? Will any of the people in Israel? Will any of the attacking army?

Joel's Prophecy: Past and Future

4. Joel 2:12-17

We now come to the second half of the structure given for Joel 1:14 - 3:21.

2:12,13a	**People:** Call to fast	
2:13b	Reason	
2:14		Consequences
2:15-17a	**Priests:** Call to blow the trumpet	
2:17b	Reason	
2:18-3:21		Consequences

Joel 2:12: "Even now," declares the LORD, "return to me with all your heart, with fasting and weeping and mourning."

Having painted the picture of the future vast, disciplined and totally destructive army of Satan on the one hand and the numberless, great and powerful army of the Lord on the other; having shown the people that whatever will confront them ... the Lord, Jehovah, is able to protect them — Joel then returns to his time. He focuses his people's mind on their present predicament with the call:

> "Even now", declares the Lord,
> "return to Me with all your heart,
> with fasting and weeping and mourning." (*NIV*)

Don't wait for such a disaster before you turn to God — do it now! EVEN NOW! With such words, with a jolt, Joel brings the people back to their present time. He wants a 100% commitment. "With all your heart" is but an echo of the Mosaic law, (Deuteronomy 6:5 and 11:13). The thought, which is always behind this phrase, is the totality of the response. When the Bible uses 'heart' it means man's thinking power, his mind. It does not mean his emotions. Thus Joel is demanding a complete change of mind and an active decision for total commitment.

Joel 2:13: Rend your heart and not your garments. Return to the LORD your God, for he is gracious and compassionate, slow to anger and abounding in love, and he relents from sending calamity.

This next verse emphasizes this further with "rend your hearts and not your garments". This repentance must be inward, with sincerity of heart; not merely an outward, symbolic exhibition. Such external shows mean nothing. Mere outward displays, not accompanied by an inward change, was the condition of the people of Jerusalem and Judah when Isaiah began to prophecy, and what the Lord thought of such a situation is adequately described in Isaiah 1:2-31.

Joel further encourages repentance by reminding the people of God's character:

> ... for He is gracious and merciful, slow to anger, and of great kindness, and repenteth Him of the evil. (*KJV*)

> ... for He is gracious and compassionate, slow to anger and abounding in love, and He relents from sending calamity. (*NIV*)

Descriptions of God as gracious and merciful come from His own words to Moses in Exodus 34:5,6. The *KJV* "great kindness" is perhaps too meek an expression. "Abounding in love" (*NIV*) or "Rich in love" (*Moffatt*) are better but the *RSV* is the strongest; "Abounding in steadfast love". This was the love He had for His people. It was this love which gave and maintained the covenants which culminated in the New Covenant (Jeremiah 31:31-34). It was this type of love He longed for in the people of Israel but all too often He found nothing more than empty ritualistic worship.

> For I desire mercy, not sacrifice, and acknowledgment of God rather than burnt offerings. (Hosea 6:6; and see again Isaiah 1:2-31.)

The expression "repenteth Him of evil" (Joel 2:13; *KJV*) is perhaps perplexing for some. How can God do evil in the first place, let alone repent of it? The expression is but a figure of speech and when used of God simply means that He will not carry out a threatened judgment, either because of intercessory prayer (see Amos 7:5) or because of a change of heart in the people involved — as possible here. The *NIV* has "relents from sending calamity", which makes this clear.

Joel 2:14: Who knows? He may turn and have pity and leave behind a blessing - grain offerings and drink offerings for the LORD your God.

So the people are called to fast and turn to the Lord because of His grace and mercy and steadfast love. In verse 14 Joel seems to pose a rhetorical question about the possible consequences if such an action was taken. Again the idea of God "repenting" comes up and here we may learn much from Amos 7:1-6. Amos received a vision of what God was thinking of doing but his prayers (Amos 7:2 and 4) persuaded God to "repent" (Amos 7:3,6) and not follow that course of action. Thus Joel implies that God's immediate actions depended upon what the people did.

The balance between God's sovereignty and man's free will is indeed difficult and not the subject of these writings. Let it be said that God is working to a predetermined plan and purpose which nothing can thwart but because He is almighty, He is able to get from most points in His plan to the next by an array of pathways. Satan may try and block some of these, and man's actions may thwart others, but they cannot block them all. Joel states that if these people will turn to God and rend their hearts then He will "turn and have pity" (*NIV*).

In Jonah 3 the Gentile King of Nineveh commanded his people to turn "from their evil ways" and stated ...

> "Who knows? God may yet relent and with compassion turn from his fierce anger so that we will not perish." (Jonah 3:9)

God did not cause the proposed judgment to fall upon that pagan city. Would these people, the ones to whom Joel was sent, the Jews of

Jerusalem and Judea, would these people repent and turn to God? To encourage them even further Joel develops his rhetorical hypothesis with:

> Who knows? He may ... leave behind a blessing - grain offerings and drink offerings for the LORD your God.

The reference to the Lord leaving behind a blessing would suggest that Joel was thinking that the Lord would miraculously step in and restore the land to provide a new harvest. "Blessings" and "harvest" would be linked in the minds of these people as indicated in Isaiah 65:8.

> "As when juice is still found in a cluster of grapes and men say, 'Don't destroy it, there is yet some good in it,' so will I do in behalf of my servants; I will not destroy them all."

If another harvest did come about then the people would again be able to go to the priest with their offerings — including the grain and drink offerings. If the people did repent, turn and rend their hearts, the subsequent blessing is likened not only to the restoration of the land from drought, locusts and fire, but also to the restoration of the people's access to God through their acceptable worship, part of which was the grain and drink offerings.

Joel 2:15: Blow the trumpet in Zion, declare a holy fast, call a sacred assembly.

Here, in verse 15, we have the second call to blow the trumpet. Those who know how much this instrument figures in the book of Revelation will not be surprised if it isn't long before Joel is again dealing with future issues, but before he does that we should note that Joel is calling everyone. No one is to be left out.

Joel 2:16: Gather the people, consecrate the assembly; bring together the elders, gather the children, those nursing at the breast. Let the bridegroom leave his room and the bride her chamber.

Here Joel seems to become more urgent that earlier (2:1), realizing the importance of what he is about to say. One can sense this from the short, sharp statements of this verse:

> Gather the people,
>> sanctify the congregation,
>>> assemble the elders,
>>>> gather the children,
>>>>> those nursing at the breast. (*KJV*)

Short, snappy orders! This urgency can be felt by the call not only to children, but even to babies and their nursing mothers. However, the most clearly seen symbol of how desperate a situation this is, is seen by the call for the bride and the groom. If the trumpet was sounded because of the presence of an "ordinary" enemy and for a "normal" war, the groom would not be "called up" for a year (Deuteronomy 24:5). Also the references to the chamber and closet and bridal canopy suggest even "newly-weds"; even those on their wedding day. Such is Joel's urgency for here he has in mind, once again, the Day of the Lord. Matthew 24 helpfully describes some of the problems of this future time, and mentions nursing mothers.

> "So when you see standing in the holy place 'the abomination that causes desolation,' spoken of through the prophet Daniel - let the reader understand - then let those who are in Judea flee to the mountains. Let no one on the roof of his house go down to take anything out of the house. Let no one in the field go back to get his cloak. How dreadful it will be in those days for pregnant women and nursing mothers! Pray that your flight will not take place in winter or on the Sabbath. For then there will be great distress, unequalled from the beginning of the world until now - and never to be equalled again. If those days had not been cut short, no one would survive, but for the sake of the elect those days will be shortened." (Matthew 24:15-22)

"Sanctify a fast" (*KJV*; verse 15) and "sanctify the congregation" (*KJV; verse 16*) are both open to misunderstanding. Like the word 'holy' the word 'sanctify' is often incorrectly understood. In fact these two words are closely connected. 'Holy' is *qodesh* and to 'sanctify' is *qadesh*. 'Holy' means set apart for God and to 'sanctify' means to set aside for sacred purposes, that is to consecrate, and the *NIV* has "consecrate the assembly" in verse 16. Exodus 19:10,22 is helpful where we can see it means to make ceremonially clean with respect to the Mosaic Law and this, perhaps, is its most common usage in the Old Testament, and this is what Joel wanted from the whole assembly.

Joel 2:17: Let the priests, who minister before the LORD, weep between the temple porch and the altar. Let them say, "Spare your people, O LORD. Do not make your inheritance an object of scorn, a byword among the nations. Why should they say among the peoples, 'Where is their God?'"

The priests and ministers of the Lord are told to "weep between the temple porch and the altar". We include a diagram of the Temple to show where this would be.

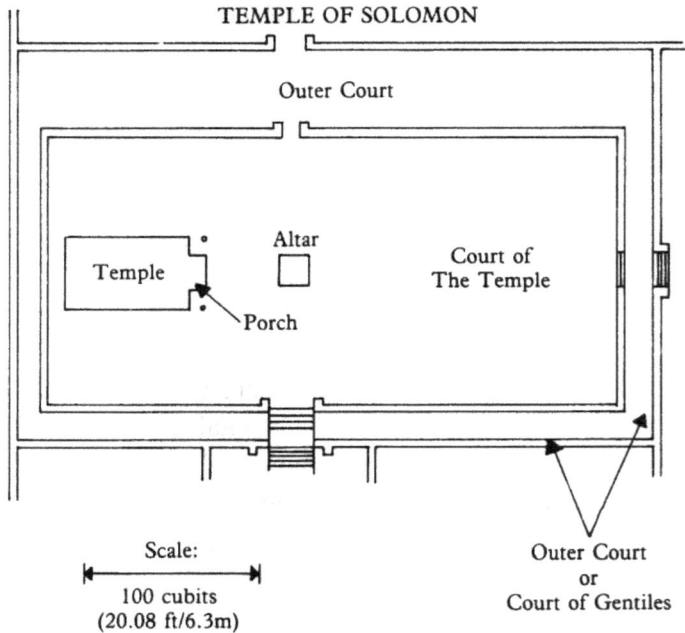

TEMPLE OF SOLOMON

Outer Court

Temple

Altar

Porch

Court of
The Temple

Scale:
100 cubits
(20.08 ft/6.3m)

Outer Court
or
Court of Gentiles

These priests are told not only to weep but also to pray and they are told what to pray:

> "Spare your people, O LORD. Do not make your inheritance an object of scorn, a byword among the nations. Why should they [the Gentile nations] say among the peoples, 'Where is their God?'"

"Thine heritage" (*KJV*), "Your inheritance" (*NIV*) is a reference to the people of Israel (Deuteronomy 32:9) and the great concern is that "the heathen should rule over them" (*KJV*). In most translations this is replaced by the expression "a byword among the nations" (*JND*; *NIV*; *Moffat*; *RSV*) and a byword is an uncomplimentary proverb about a place, a people or a person, which has something bad about it.

> "Do not make your inheritance ... a byword among the nations." (*NIV*)

There is the call to blow the trumpets and the priests are called to weep and pray because Joel is concerned about the nations mocking Israel and doubting the existence of their God. "Why should the nations sneer, Where is their God?" is *Moffatt*'s effective translation.

5. Joel 2:18-20

Sooner or later one would expect the sneering challenge "Where is their God?" to be loudly and clearly answered by the Lord. The consequences of this derisory remark fill the rest of this prophecy, that is Joel 2:18 - 3:21, and make up the last member of the structure given at the start of this study. However, to help us deal with what follows we construct a structure for these remaining verses of Joel.

2:18,19	Good bestowed	Land and people
2:20	Evil removed	Enemy cut off
2:21-32	Good bestowed	Land and people
3:1-16a	Evil removed	Enemy cut off
3:16b-18	Good bestowed	Land and people
3:19	Evil removed	Enemy cut off
3:20,21	Good bestowed	Land and people

Joel 2:18: Then the LORD will be jealous for his land and take pity on his people.

What are to be the consequences of such a sneer as "Where is their God?" We live in the dispensation of the fulness of God's grace and nowadays many sneer at our gracious God, but at this future time, during this Day of the Lord, when Israel's very existence is threatened and God's promises to them are in jeopardy ... what will He do?

> *Then* will the Lord be jealous for *His* land, and pity *His* people. (Joel 2:18, *KJV*)

The land referred to here is Jerusalem and the surrounding countryside, Judea. That land is in much dispute today and will continue to be so right up to and through this Day of the Lord. It is salutary to appreciate that "the heavens are" God's but so too is the earth (Psalm 89:11). If he has decided to give a certain part of it to a particular people

(Genesis 15:18), then none can object and, in fulfilment of that promise, the people of Israel must, one day in the future, receive it *all* and dwell in it.

The word 'jealous', *qanna,* is better translated 'zealous' when applied to God. It is intended to show that He is not an abstract entity, neither an impersonal force or a cold being, but a living, personal, loving God Whose love is intense and exclusive in the sense that it does not tolerate rival gods (Exodus 20:5). It is because He is the living, personal God Who is zealous, that Proverbs 3:11,12 records that "the Lord disciplines those He loves". Every father knows that his children need discipline administered in love, and Joel's prophecy deals with the disciplining of Jerusalem and Judea.

Joel 2:19: The LORD will reply to them: "I am sending you grain, new wine and oil, enough to satisfy you fully; never again will I make you an object of scorn to the nations."

The Lord now speaks and promises that there will be a time when He will send the grain and the wine and the people shall be "satisfied". The *NIV* puts it more strongly than the *KJV,* saying He will send "enough to satisfy you fully", and *Moffatt* has "till you have ample". These show that the Lord will indeed be bountiful and how He accomplishes this is explained more fully in Joel 2:21-27 which we shall consider later.

However as well as restoring the grain, the wine and the oil to such an extent that the people will be more than satisfied, the Lord tells them that they shall no longer "be taunted by the pagans" (*Moffatt*); they shall never again be "an object of scorn to the nations" (*NIV*). In such passages as Jeremiah 9:13-16 and 13:22-24, the Lord promised that if they forsook Him He would scatter them amongst the nations but Ezekiel 11:17 looks to the same time as Joel 2:19. In these God promises that He will gather them from these nations and give them the land of Israel; (see also Matthew 24:31).

Joel 2:20: "I will drive the northern army far from you, pushing it into a parched and barren land, with its front columns going into the

**eastern sea and those in the rear into the western sea. And its stench
will go up; its smell will rise." Surely he has done great things.**

How will God set about achieving these promises? First by removing the
evil and, in particular, the enemy described in Joel 2:20. In the *KJV* you
will note that the word army is in italics. This signifies that in the original
Hebrew there was no word for 'army' but the translators felt a word
needed to be supplied for the English to be clear. Certainly it would be a
good idea if all translations followed this practice and then everyone
could see what the translators have added.

The *RSV* translators felt no need to supply an extra word; "I will remove
the northerner far from you". Other translations are:

> "The foe from the north I will drive out." (*Moffatt*)
> "I will remove the northern peril far away from you." (*NEB*)
> "I will drive the northern army far from *you*." (*NIV*)

Perhaps the most significant translation of this verse is supplied by
J.N. Darby:

> "I will remove far from you him that cometh from the north."

With reference to verse 20 in the *KJV* we read "drive *him*", "*his* face",
"*his* hinder part", "*his* stink", "*his* ill savour" and "*he* hath done", a
singular noun, rather than a collective one, would best fit the context and
the translator's need. However, the *NIV* in all these verses has the
impersonal 'its' in Joel 2:20, but then reverts to the personal 'he' at the
end of the verse.

Who is this northern army? Who is this northerner? The army has been
described in Joel 2:2-10 but who is its leader? Some claim that Joel 2:2-10
and verse 20 refer to nothing more than a plague of locusts but not only
do such verses as 2:7 and 8 make this highly unlikely, verse 20 makes it
impossible. Locusts do not attack the land of Israel from the north. Thus
who is this northerner?

Daniel 11 is a difficult chapter and at verse 21 there is a distinct break. The first 20 verses may now be history but we read that "a contemptible person" is to arise, "a vile person" (Daniel 11:21; *NIV* & *KJV*). These words herald in the still future "king of the north". The whole of Daniel 11:21-45 is about the exploits of this future king of the north and a future king of the south — with the people of Israel stuck in the middle. It helps in understanding these passages to remember that north and south are with respect to Jerusalem and the land of Judea. All nations entering Israel "on foot" must enter either from the north or from the south. Who is this king of the north? Who is this king of the south? There was, and still is, only one nation near Israel to the south and that is Egypt. Thus many agree that the king of the south is Egypt but ... The king of the north? Which is that? To answer would require another book! Suffice it to say that there are several nations near to the land of Israel which would have to use the northern route. Even Babylon, which was to the east of Judea, came from the north when they conquered it. However, it is one of these nations, but which one is *not* clearly revealed in Scripture. A detailed study will narrow down the possibilities but those alive in that day, during that Day of the Lord, will have no doubts; they will know.

Note that Daniel 11:36 says that this king of the north "will do as he pleases. He will exalt and magnify himself above every god and will say unheard-of things against the God of gods. He will be successful until ..." (*NIV*). He "shall do according to his will; and he shall exalt himself, and *magnify himself* **above** every God, and shall speak marvellous things against the God of gods and shall prosper till ..." (*KJV*).

In Joel 2:20 the expression "he has done great things" can be translated "he *magnified himself* to do great things". This expression occurs also in Daniel 8 where this same being is termed the "little horn" but he doesn't stay little for long!

> ... a little horn which waxed exceeding great, towards the south, and towards the east and towards the pleasant land. And it waxed great, even to the host of heaven, and it cast down some of the host and of the stars to the ground and stamped upon

them. Yea, he *magnified himself* even to the prince of the host, and by him the daily sacrifice was taken away, and the place of His sanctuary was cast down. (Daniel 8:9-11 *KJV*)

Our studies so far in Joel allow us to appreciate, but not savour, those words in Daniel 8 and 11 but let us be thankful that we stopped in the middle of a sentence in Daniel 11:36.

He will be successful *until* the time of wrath is completed, for what has been determined must take place.

He shall prosper for a time but then he shall be defeated and Joel reveals the extent of that defeat. The Lord says:

"I will drive the northern army far from you, pushing it into a parched and barren land, with its front columns going into the eastern sea and those in the rear into the western sea. And its stench will go up; its smell will rise." (Joel 2:20)

How will this defeat of the king of the north, this "little horn" who is backed by Satan (Daniel 11:38,39; Revelation 13:4), be accomplished? It is interesting to note that just as Satan has many names (e.g. the dragon, the serpent, the devil etc.) so too has this puppet of his. Paul describes him as:

The man of lawlessness is revealed, the man doomed to destruction. He will oppose and will exalt himself over everything that is called God or is worshipped, so that he sets himself up in God's temple, proclaiming himself to be God. (2 Thessalonians 2:3-4; *NIV*)

The man of sin, the son of perdition, who opposeth and exalteth himself above all that is called God or that is worshipped: so that he as God sitteth in the Temple of God, showing himself that he is God. (2 Thessalonians 2:3-4; *KJV*)

So this army of Joel 2:2-10 manages to overrun the land of Israel, take

Jerusalem and occupy the Temple. Satan manages to acquire, via this being of his, the worship he so badly wants.

> Men worshipped the dragon [Satan] because he had given authority to the beast [another name for this king of the north], and they also worshipped the beast." (Revelation 13:4)

The extent of that worship is "All inhabitants of the earth will worship the beast" (Revelation 13:8). However, the word translated 'earth' in this verse is the Greek *ge* (which corresponds to the Hebrew *erets*) and which is elsewhere translated 'land' or 'country'. It occurs many times in Revelation and is mostly translated 'earth'.

From Joel, and elsewhere, we see it is the Jews in Jerusalem and Judea who are made to worship this beast (e.g. see Matthew 24:15-24).

This is accomplished with the help of another being, "another beast" (Revelation 13:11) who is usually termed the "false prophet" (Revelation 16:13). His exploits are fully described in Revelation 13:11-18. We read:

> Because of the signs he was given power to do on behalf of the first beast, he deceived the inhabitants of the earth. He ordered them to set up an image in honor of the beast who was wounded by the sword and yet lived. (Revelation 13:14)

Again, 'earth' is best understood to mean the 'land' of Judea or the 'country' of Israel, for the image is to be set up in the temple in Jerusalem (2 Thessalonians 2:4).

Will God tolerate this for long? Thankfully not! For at *most* 42 months[4] Satan, his beast and his false prophet will enjoy success but then:

---

[4] 42 months is a period of three and a half years, half of seven years, a time a times and half a time, 1,260 days; common expressions in prophecy relating to the 42 months just prior to the return of Christ.

And then the lawless one will be revealed, whom the Lord Jesus will overthrow with the breath of his mouth and destroy by the splendor of his coming. The coming of the lawless one will be in accordance with the work of Satan displayed in all kinds of counterfeit miracles, signs and wonders. (2 Thessalonians 2:8-9)

Many passages of Scripture can throw light upon this tremendous event. Zechariah 14:1-11 is well worth reading and states that "then will the Lord go out and fight". Matthew 24:1-31 is another valuable passage describing that time in Jerusalem and Judea as a "great distress, unequalled from the beginning of the world until now - and never to be equaled again". And it goes on to say, "If those days had not been cut short, no one would survive" (verses 21-22). In his desperate attempt to wipe out the Jew, it appears Satan might be prepared to wipe out humanity, but God steps in. However, Matthew 24:22 may be simply referring to the Jews, to those living in Jerusalem and Judea.

What a tremendous day that will be when God, in the person of Christ, breaks into the world again. Revelation 19:11-21 tries to describe that day but it is far from easy to understand. We could go on for much longer but perhaps we have thrown enough light on Joel 2:20 and what is behind the expression:

> "I will remove from you him that cometh from the north." (Joel 2:20 *JND*)

6. Joel 2:21-32

We now come to the central part of Joel's prophecy and will, in this study, deal with the longest section of the one entitled "Good bestowed; land and people". To help us we set out the following structure:

2: 21-27 Temporal gifts and signs
2:21a   Words to the soil
  2.21b   Reason
2:22a   Words to the beasts
  2:22b   Reason
2:23a   Words to the people
  2:23a-27   Reason

2:28-32 Spiritual gifts and signs
2:28,29   Afterwards: Pour out My spirit
  2:30,31   Before: Wonders in heaven
2:32   Afterwards: Deliverance.

The return of Christ, merely alluded to in Joel 2:20, heralds in a time when "The Lord will be King over the whole earth" (Zechariah 14:9). However we must remember that His Kingship will not be immediately acknowledged. Initially He is to rule with a rod of iron (Psalm 2:5-9) and this is understandable if we appreciate what the world is to become like. Also what the world would have just gone through. Revelation 13 gives us that sad picture of what faces Israel, from one point of view, and Matthew 24:21 describes that time as "a great tribulation, such as was not since the beginning of the world to this time, no, nor ever shall be" (*KJV*).

Joel 2:21: Be not afraid, O land; be glad and rejoice. Surely the LORD has done great things.

After the great battle, swiftly passed over by Joel in 2:20, there will be the need of food for the animals and the people. It is not surprising, therefore, that the first words of the Lord are addressed to the soil *(adamah)* which is told not to fear because He, the Lord, will do great things. What exactly — we are not immediately told.

Joel 2:22: Be not afraid, O wild animals, for the open pastures are becoming green. The trees are bearing their fruit; the fig tree and the vine yield their riches.

Then the animals are told not to be afraid for the land is recovering.

Joel 2:23: Be glad, O people of Zion, rejoice in the LORD your God, for he has given you the autumn rains in righteousness. He sends you abundant showers, both autumn and spring rains, as before.

Then, the people of Zion, are told to rejoice in the Lord their God. They have just been saved from destruction at the hand of the king of the north and the One Who saved them was the One their forefathers crucified! On that day "They will look on me, the one they have pierced" and the realization that, as a nation, they have rejected him throughout the centuries leads, understandably, to a great period of mourning (Zechariah 12:9-10; see also Revelation 1:7).

After that the people turn their attention to the land and see it desolate. However they are told to rejoice in the Lord their God. He will cure this land, but how? How will it recover? How will He cause it to flourish during His reign on earth? The answer may lie in such passages as Leviticus 26:3,4. There the people of Israel are told:

> "If you follow my decrees and are careful to obey my commands, I will send you rain in its season, and the ground will yield its crops and the trees of the field their fruit."

When is this "due season" for the land of Israel? Deuteronomy 11:13,14 supplies the answer:

Joel's Prophecy: Past and Future

"So if you faithfully obey the commands I am giving you today - to love the LORD your God and to serve him with all your heart and with all your soul - then I will send rain on your land in its season, both autumn and spring rains, so that you may gather in your grain, new wine and oil."

Such passages as these[5], and also Hosea 6:3 and Jeremiah 5:24, may have been in Joel's mind. This first, or early, rain falls during October and November and enables the ground to be prepared for the seeds. The normal rainy season is December to February but the latter rain is to fall in March and April, bringing on the harvest. Without such latter rain the harvest is poor. At present it is the restoration of this latter rain that parts of the land of Israel so desperately needs if it is to be bountiful. The many irrigation schemes, now undertaken in that part of the world, will not be necessary when the latter rain is restored by the Lord after His Second Coming.

This kingdom which He is to set up on earth, has Christ reigning from Jerusalem (Isaiah 2:1-4). It is a time when the wolf will feed 'with' the lamb, and not 'on' the lamb (Isaiah 11:6; 65:25). Longevity will return, but it is not a perfect paradise; there will still be sin (Isaiah 65:20). This kingdom is to last for 1,000 years, (Revelation 20:2) during which time Satan is to be bound and will be prevented from interfering with mankind.

Some think that this will be a time of perfection and sinlessness but, as mentioned above, this is not so. Not all of man's sins are due to Satan (Matthew 15:19) and we have read that at the start of this kingdom the Lord is to rule with a rod of iron and Isaiah 65:20 indicates sin is still present. However it is to be the most blessed time on earth and it is often called the Millennial Kingdom or simply, the Millennium — which is the Latin word for 1,000.

Before moving on — just one further point. In Joel 2:23 the *KJV* has the

---

[5] See also Deuteronomy 28:1-14 and also *Deuteronomy 28: A Key to Understanding* by Michael Penny, published by The Open Bible Trust.

former rain 'moderately', which might suggest that the Lord is not giving as much as He could. *JND* has "the early rain in *due* measure". The Lord is to give the due measure, the correct proportion for the abundant fertility of the seeds; not too much — not too little. The *NIV* has 'abundant' showers.

Joel 2:24: The threshing floors will be filled with grain; the vats will overflow with new wine and oil.

All is set up in the kingdom in which "The wolf and the lamb will feed together, and the lion will eat straw like the ox" (Isaiah 65:25). The reference in this verse of Isaiah to the serpent eating dust may well be an allegorical representation of Satan being bound for the 1,000 year duration of that kingdom (Revelation 20:2; and note Genesis 3:14).

Joel 2:25: "I will repay you for the years the locusts have eaten - the great locust and the young locust, the other locusts and the locust swarm - my great army that I sent among you."

In Joel 2:23-25 the people are told to be glad and they certainly have much to be glad about. Verse 24 states that "The threshing floors will be filled with grain; the vats will overflow with new wine and oil." No problem now with the grain and drink offerings. Not only are the offerings restored but verse 25 sees the restoration of *everything* to Israel. Everything that was lost to the locusts is restored. Everything that was lost to that great army is restored. No wonder they are told to rejoice and be glad.

Some people have a problem with the words "My great army which I sent among you". Did God directly cause this catastrophe? No! But because He is the omnipotent, the all-powerful One Who can *do* anything and Who can *stop* anything, He could have stopped the ravaging locusts and He could have stopped that great army of Joel 2:2-10, even before it had embarked upon its mission — but He chose not to. Because He didn't, because He allowed it, He takes the responsibility and so calls the plague of locusts "*my* great army". Any catastrophe He allows His people to go through is fully noted by Him and He, the righteous One, will *more than* compensate them for their suffering with blessings either in this life or after resurrection (Romans 8:18 and 2 Corinthians 4:17 show Paul appreciated this point).

Another example of this is found in the opening chapters of Job where Satan wished to inflict hardship upon Job and his family (Job 1:1-11). The Lord *allowed* Satan to do this (1:12) but later, in Job 2:3, God himself took the responsibility for those sufferings upon His own shoulders. The last chapter of Job then shows how the Lord more than compensated Job for what He had permitted Job to undergo.

Joel 2:26-27: You will have plenty to eat, until you are full, and you will praise the name of the LORD your God, who has worked wonders for you; never again will my people be shamed. Then you will know that I am in Israel, that I am the LORD your God, and that there is no other; never again will my people be shamed.

This section of the structure closes with verses 26 and 27. The people are told that they "will praise the name of the Lord" and that they will know that He is in the midst of them. There are also two references, one in verse 26 *and* one in verse 27, to:

> "My people shall never be ashamed." (*KJV*)
> "Never again shall My people be put to shame." (*NIV*)
> "Never again shall My people be derided." (Moffatt)

This event sees the fulfilment of the promise of Deuteronomy 28:13:

> The LORD will make you the head, not the tail. If you pay attention to the commands of the LORD your God that I give you this day and carefully follow them, you will always be at the top, never at the bottom.

Many of the promises to the people of Israel are conditional upon the behaviour of that people. Deuteronomy 28:13, above, has "if you pay attention to the commands of the Lord." Similar conditions are found in such passages as Leviticus 26:3,4 and Deuteronomy 11:13,14. However there is a time coming when this people will hearken and will obey. It will be after those days when they shall "look on Him Whom they pierced". It shall be in those days after the return of Christ. Jeremiah 31:31-34 records that:

> "The time is coming," declares the LORD, "when I will make a new covenant with the house of Israel and with the house of Judah. It will not be like the covenant I made with their forefathers when I took them by the hand to lead them out of Egypt, because they broke my covenant, though I was a husband to them," declares the LORD.
>
> "This is the covenant I will make with the house of Israel after that time," declares the LORD. "I will put my law in their minds and write it on their hearts. I will be their God, and they will be my people. No longer will a man teach his neighbour, or a man his brother, saying, 'Know the LORD,' because they will all know me, from the least of them to the greatest," declares the LORD. "For I will forgive their wickedness and will remember their sins no more."

Such is the hope of the house of Israel and the house of Judah (Jeremiah 31:31). Ezekiel 11:19,20 adds further light:

> "I will give them an undivided heart and put a new spirit in them; I will remove from them their heart of stone and give them a heart of flesh. Then they will follow my decrees and be careful to keep my laws. They will be my people, and I will be their God."

This comes after the gathering of the people to the land the Lord has given them (Ezekiel 11:17-20,) and Ezekiel 37:1-14 shows that the two nations, the northern kingdom of Israel and the southern kingdom of Judah, these two become one. This gathering takes place after the return of the Lord to the earth (Matthew 24:29-31; Zechariah 12:9-14).

Joel 2:28-29: "And afterwards, I will pour out my Spirit on all people. Your sons and daughters will prophesy, your old men will dream dreams, your young men will see visions. Even on my

servants, both men and women, I will pour out my Spirit in those days."

Ezekiel 11:17-20 covers, only more briefly, what is written about in Joel 2:21-29 and makes clear one point which has perplexed some people. The passage from Ezekiel makes it clear that "I will put a new spirit within you" (verse 19, *KJV*) comes after the people of Israel have been gathered into the land (verse 17) — and this gathering, we have seen, comes *after* the Lord's return. And this is precisely what Joel 2:28 states; *"afterwards, I will pour out my spirit on all people"*

From these verses alone, taken out of their context, we may be left asking "afterwards?" After what? After the ravaging of Satan's army in Joel 2:2-10? After the northern enemy had been destroyed by the Lord's coming (Joel 2:20)? After the good bestowed upon the land, the animals and the people (Joel 2:21-27)? Yes! After all these have taken place. After the Lord's return; after the nation had been gathered into the land; after the land had been blessed with the latter rain; after the good bestowed had begun to be enjoyed — then ... then "I will pour out my spirit on all people" (Joel 2:28). "I will pour out my spirit in those days"(Joel 2:29). Other passages, such as Ezekiel 37:1-14 and Zechariah 12:9-14, add details but from all such passages it is clear that the pouring out of the spirit upon these people comes after the Lord's return.

Passages such as Joel 2:28,29 and Jeremiah 31:31-34 etc. bring us to one of the high water marks of the Old Testament. God had desired that *all* the people of Israel would be mouthpieces and prophets for Him (Numbers 11:29). His wish was that they would be a kingdom of Priests (Exodus 19:6) and, as such, take the message of His plan and purpose of salvation for mankind to all nations of the world. This desire, this wish, shall be realized in the Millennium when "the earth will be full of the knowledge of the Lord as the waters cover the sea" (Isaiah 11:9). The knowledge He is to give to Israel and Judah (Jeremiah 31:31-34), they will pass on to all nations, so fulfilling their role as a kingdom of priests.

One point in Joel 2:28,29 which we might easily pass over is that the spirit is to be poured out on *all* people, and in the context of Joel this would mean all Israel. This would be very important to those in the Old Testament times. It is difficult for us who have been sealed, when we believed the gospel of Salvation and were sealed with the Holy Spirit until the day of redemption (Ephesians 1:13 and 4:30), and who have been strengthened by His Spirit in the inner man (Ephesians 3:16), and who can be filled by the Spirit (Ephesians 5:18), to appreciate that the Comforter has not always been available to all people for all the time. Suffice it to say that in those Old Testament times the Holy Spirit was generally given to only a few people and often for only a limited time. It was to enable them to carry out God's will —whatever that may have been.

During the construction of the Tabernacle or the building of the Temple some craftsmen were endowed with special skills and abilities, thus producing extremely beautiful work but ... whatever that work was, when it had been completed, the Holy Spirit left them.

Again God could remove His Holy Spirit if the person sinned badly and He did this to Saul, and David was afraid God might do the same to him. Hence David's great plea in Psalm 51:11 "Do not take your Holy Spirit from me!" Thus the promise that God's Holy Spirit was to be poured out "upon all people" was of great significance to those alive in Joel's time.

There is little more to say on these two verses other than to point out that *to prophesy* does not necessarily mean to foretell the future. To prophesy means to speak things about God — His character, His being, His past activities, His present purpose and, if necessary, His future plans. In these two verses Joel has definitely been speaking about the future, about what is to happen to the people of Israel after Christ returns.

Joel 2:30-31: I will show wonders in the heavens and on the earth, blood and fire and billows of smoke. The sun will be turned to darkness and the moon to blood before the coming of the great and dreadful day of the LORD.

Joel 2:28-31 contain two groups of seven items. The first seven take place after the return of Christ; the second seven take place before. It may be profitable to display them:

"And **AFTERWARD,**

I will pour out my Spirit on   all people.
                                     Your sons
                                     and daughters will prophesy,
                                     your old men will dream dreams,
                                     your young men will see visions.
                                     Even on my servants,
                                     both men and women,
I will pour out my Spirit in those days.

I will show wonders   in the heavens and
                                     on the earth,
                                     blood and
                                     fire and
                                     billows of smoke.
                                     The sun will be turned to darkness and
                                     the moon to blood
BEFORE the coming of the great and dreadful day of the LORD."

To miss the 'before' in verse 31 can cause much confusion. Some seem to think that the wonders in heaven etc. come *after* the pouring out of the Spirit but that is to misread Joel. The pouring out of the Spirit comes 'afterwards' and although it may not be clear to us exactly how long 'after' the Lord's return that pouring out will be, none the less we do know it is 'after' that great event.

Similarly we may not know for how long 'before' the Lord's return these wonders in the heaven and earth, will last, but we do know these events take place 'before' His return and that these difficult and depressing days are brought to a close by His return. However, Matthew 24 makes it clear that after the distressing Day of the Lord, and just before Christ's return, there will be signs in the heavens.

"Immediately after the distress of those days 'the sun will be darkened, and the moon will not give its light; the stars will fall from the sky, and the heavenly bodies will be shaken.' At that time the sign of the Son of Man will appear in the sky." (Matthew 24:29-30)

Joel 2:30-32 takes us back in time to before Joel 2:28,29; to before the events described in Joel 2:21-27. It takes us to just after those days described in Joel 2:2-11 and possibly 2:20.

Reading again Joel 2:30-31, and other passages like Matthew 24:29, one wonders how can these things be? How is it possible? How will it happen? What will be the mechanics? We don't know. We are not told. Even if we were told we probably wouldn't (couldn't) understand.

Also, as we read such passages again, we may well ask "what *exactly* are the astronomical events described in Joel 2:30,31?" Again, we cannot be definite. Those alive at this future time will have no trouble in seeing *exactly* what these words depict. Matthew 24:21 describes those days as a "great distress, unequalled from the beginning of the world until now - and never to be equalled again." Joel's prophecy, to such as know it, will be a great comfort to those living during that time.

Joel 2:32: And everyone who calls on the name of the LORD will be saved; for on Mount Zion and in Jerusalem there will be deliverance, as the LORD has said, among the survivors whom the LORD calls.

Remembering that we are now back to "the great and terrible Day of the Lord" which precedes Christ's return, we ask what is this deliverance which will be provided in Jerusalem and the surrounding country? Deliverance is *peletah* which is translated elsewhere "escape". Remnant is not the usual word *(she'erith)* but is *sariyd,* a derivative of *sarad* which means a "survivor". Thus *sariyd* means "those left" or "that which remains". Matthew 24:15-21 exhorts those who are alive in Judea to flee into the mountains and Revelation 12 states that there they shall be fed (verses 6 and 14) and protected (verse 16) by God for 1260 days, three and a half years. This is the deliverance of Joel 2:32.

Joel's Prophecy: Past and Future

7. Joel 3:1-21

Joel 2:15-17 records the call to blow the trumpet and has an exhortation for the priests to pray to the Lord so that the heathen would not rule over Israel and the nations would not sneer "where is their God?". The rest of Joel (2:18-3:2 1) deals with the consequences of this action and its structure is:

2:18,19	Good bestowed; land and people
2:20	Evil removed. Enemy cut off
2:21-32	Good bestowed; land and people
3:1-16a	Evil removed, Enemy cut off
3:16b-18	Good bestowed; land and people
3:19	Evil removed. Enemy cut off
3:20,21	Good bestowed; land and people.

We have already dealt with the third member of the above structure; the longest one dealing with the "Good bestowed". Now we turn to the fourth member, the longest dealing with the "evil removed". Its structure is as follows:

3:1,2a	Gathering
3:2b	Place and Act. "I will judge".
3:3-8	Judgment threatened
3:9-12a	Gathering
3:12b	Place and Act. "I will judge"
3:13	Judgment executed
3:14a	Gathering
3:14b	Place and Act. Valley of judgment
3:15-16a	Judgment threatened.

Joel 3:1: In those days and at that time, when I restore the fortunes of Judah and Jerusalem.

The opening words of chapter 3 should make us stop and ask to which point in time is Joel referring? Is it those days of Joel 2:30-32 or some other time? When is the time that the Lord will "restore the fortunes of Judah and Jerusalem?" Clearly 'those days' follow on from the days of Joel 2:32.

However, before we move on, it may help some if we look at a problem caused by this verse given in the *KJV*. There we read:

> "For, behold, in those days, and in that time, when I shall bring again the captivity of Judah and Jerusalem".

What does the expression "bring again the captivity" mean? Surprisingly, as we have seen from the *NIV*, it means to "restore the fortunes" or "relieve from trouble". This is clear from Amos 9:14,15:

> "And I will bring again the captivity of My people Israel, and they shall build the waste cities, and inhabit them: and they shall plant vineyards, and drink the wine thereof: they shall also make gardens, and eat the fruit of them. And I will plant them upon their land, and they shall no more be pulled up out of their land which I have given them," saith the Lord thy God. (*KJV*)

Jeremiah 30:3 is another passage which shows the meaning of this expression to be the gathering and restoring of the people of Israel to their land. There the expression is translated "When I restore the fortunes of Judah and Jerusalem" by the *NIV*, *Moffatt* and *RSV* The *NEB* translates Joel 3:1 as "when I *reverse* the fortunes of Judah and Jerusalem". The Hebrew is *shubh* which means to turn, return or turn back. So here it means to turn back the captivity; i.e. to restore the people, to reverse their fortunes. We know this reversal takes place at the Lord's Second Coming.

Joel 3:2: "I will gather all nations and bring them down to the Valley of Jehoshaphat. There I will enter into judgment against them concerning my inheritance, my people Israel, for they scattered my people among the nations and divided up my land."

So, at that time, in those days, about the time of the return of Christ the Lord states "I will gather all nations, and bring them down to the valley of Jehoshaphat". This is again mentioned in Zechariah 14:2 and the ensuing battle has been fully described in Joel 2:2-10. The second half of Zechariah 14:2 describes explicitly the events of Joel 2:9.

Again care must be exercised over the expression "I will gather all the nations to Jerusalem to fight against it" (Zechariah 14:2). Here God, once more, is taking responsibility for events which He allows. Revelation 19:19 makes it clear that behind this great battle is the beast, the king of the north, that 'little horn', and behind him is Satan.

The mention of Jehoshaphat has led some to want to date Joel's prophecy in the reign of that king (819-794 B.C.) but this is not logical. If a valley bears a king's name we can be certain that the prophecy was not written *before* that king ruled but it could have been written *any time* during or after.

The name Jehoshaphat means "Jehovah has judged" and so the valley of Jehoshaphat is a most appropriate place for this battle and ensuing judgment. Some suggest this is the Kidron valley, situated between the Mount of Olives and Jerusalem, but others dispute it.[6] Here judgment is dispensed and to here Christ returns.

> On that day his feet will stand on the Mount of Olives, east of Jerusalem. (Zechariah 14:4)

What an event that will be! How the nations will be amazed! But how they will be judged? We may not always understand God's judgments but Abraham knew that the Judge of all the earth would do right (Genesis 18:25). And we would do well always to keep in mind that He is a God of love; He is a *righteous* God and He is the *righteous* judge (2 Timothy 4:8).

---

[6] See, for example, *The Day of the Locust: Joel and the Day of the Lord* by Charles Ozanne: further details on page 106.

"I will plead with them for My people" (Joel 3:2, *KJV*) may be a little misleading. The *RSV* has "I will enter into judgment with them on account of My people and My heritage Israel". *Moffatt*, as usual, is more vivid. "I shall assign them their doom for the treatment of Israel, My heritage". Here the promise of Genesis 12:3 is to be fulfilled. There Abraham was told that:

> "I will bless those who bless you,
> and whoever curses you I will curse."

Matthew 25:31-46 also deals with the judgment of these nations. This, again, showing the still future fulfilment of Genesis 12:3 and verses 40 and 45 gives the basis of that judgment: how had the nations treated "these my brothers"; i.e. the people of Israel. One aspect of this treatment is the scattering of the people of Israel (Joel 3:2). Here again we meet with the problem of one verse saying the nations scattered Israel and another verse saying God scattered Israel. The problem is not difficult for God allowed the nations to scatter His people because of their sin and unbelief. He permitted a nation to teach Israel a lesson, to show them that He was their true God but ... how did that nation treat the people of Israel? That is the issue. That is what is to be judged.

Even today, some country's treatment of the exiled Jews leaves much to be desired and that country's leaders would do well to read Genesis 12:3.

Joel 3:2b-3: they scattered my people among the nations and divided up my land. They cast lots for my people and traded boys for prostitutes; they sold girls for wine that they might drink.

In verses 2-6, possibly to demonstrate how badly Israel had been treated by the nations, Joel gives historical examples of maltreatment. A more comprehensive list of such treatments is found in Amos 1:1-2:3, a prophecy which had been written many years before Joel.

> "for they have scattered my people throughout their own countries, have taken each their portion of my land and shared out my people by lot, bartered a boy for a whore and sold a girl

Joel's Prophecy: Past and Future

for wine and drunk it down." (Joel 3:2-3, *NEB*)

The reference to "parted my land" (*KJV* and *JND*) or "divided up my land" (*NIV*; Moffatt; *RSV*) is very significant and may be applicable to today. The present day partitioning of that land may well be an example of Joel 3:2.

Joel 3:4-8: "Now what have you against me, O Tyre and Sidon and all you regions of Philistia? Are you repaying me for something I have done? If you are paying me back, I will swiftly and speedily return on your heads what you have done. For you took my silver and my gold and carried off my finest treasures to your temples. You sold the people of Judah and Jerusalem to the Greeks, that you might send them far from their homeland.

See, I am going to rouse them out of the places to which you sold them, and I will return on your own heads what you have done. I will sell your sons and daughters to the people of Judah, and they will sell them to the Sabeans, a nation far away, the Lord has spoken."

The region termed Palestine in the *KJV* of Joel 3:4 must not be confused with modern day Palestine. Most translations, like the *NIV* above, have Philistia and this was a coastal strip of land west of Jerusalem. Tyre and Sidon were two sea ports some 100 miles or so north of that region. The following map may be of some use. It shows some of the principal places and divisions of the land which took place during the reigns of the kings of Israel and Judah.

Why Tyre and Sidon and the regions of Philistia should be singled out is not obvious. Earlier Amos (1:9-12) had accused Tyre of not remembering the brotherly covenant, which may be a reference to 2 Samuel 5:11 and 1 Kings 5:1 and 9:11-14. Ezekiel 28:24 had described Sidon as a pricking brier and a grievous thorn but he doesn't give clear indication of what he had in mind. It could be that Tyre and Sidon, together with parts of Philistia, were the haven of the wealthy slave traders. Amos 1:6-9 mentions Gaza, a port of Philistia, and links it with the slave trade. This would be in agreement with Joel 3:6.

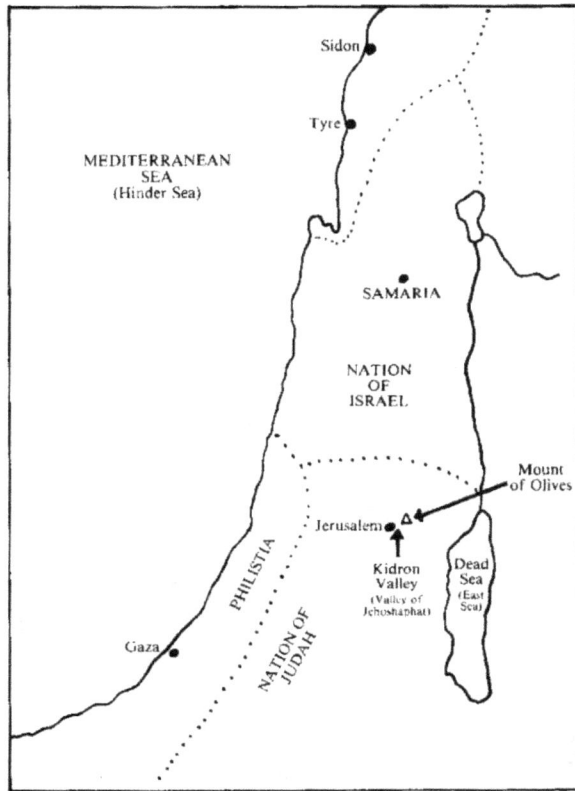

Sidon

Tyre

MEDITERRANEAN
SEA
(Hinder Sea)

SAMARIA

NATION
OF
ISRAEL

Mount
of Olives

Jerusalem

Kidron
Valley
(Valley of
Jehoshaphat)

Dead
Sea
(East
Sea)

PHILISTIA

NATION OF
JUDAH

Gaza

Scale |———| 1 cm   = 20 kilometers

|———————| 1 inch   = 33 miles

Some think that the reference to slavery shows that Joel was written after the return to the land from the Babylonian exile because Nehemiah mentions slavery in 5:5 and Tyre in 13:16. However, Nehemiah does not link Tyre with slavery, but with selling fish on the Sabbath. Also this practice of slavery had taken place on many occasions and, as we have read, Amos mentions it in 1:6-9 and that prophecy was written before the exile.

The reference to temple robbery (Joel 3:5) would also be more appropriate if placed before the exile. On returning to their homeland the people wanted to build a temple and did so, but Ezra and Nehemiah clearly indicate that it was a humble place, with none of the slendour of Solomon's temple.

Joel 3:4 finishes by stating the obvious. If they, or anyone else come to that, attempt to "get their own back" on God then He will swiftly and speedily return on their heads what they have done. In this age of grace in which we live, God is silent and stands back and takes man's abuse but then ... in that day ... in that great and terrible Day of the Lord, things will be different. This dispensation will have closed.

After the selling and scattering of the children of Judah and Jerusalem (verse 6) we get the gathering of them (verse 7). In the age of the Mosaic Law, where the rule is an eye for an eye and a tooth for a tooth, He would exercise that justice. Those who have mistreated the people in this way will be treated likewise and will be sent to a people far off. It is not certain who the Sabeans were but it is certain that the children of Judah will then be free from those who have persecuted and mistreated them.

Before moving on some may care to know that these verses, Joel 3:4-8, are the only ones which do not appear in poetic form in any of the translations which have been consulted. *Moffatt* and the *RSV* have a larger portion, Joel 3:1-8, in prose and the *ESV* has the whole of 2:30-3:8 in prose.

Joel 3:9-13: Proclaim this among the nations: Prepare for war! Rouse the warriors! Let all the fighting men draw near and attack. Beat your plowshares into swords and your pruning hooks into spears. Let the weakling say, "I am strong!" Come quickly, all you nations from every side, and assemble there. Bring down your warriors, O LORD! "Let the nations be roused; let them advance into the Valley of Jehoshaphat, for there I will sit to judge all the nations on every side. Swing the sickle, for the harvest is ripe. Come, trample the grapes, for the winepress is full and the vats overflow - so great is their wickedness!"

In Joel 3:9-12a we have the other side of verse 2. There God said "I will gather all nations" but from this section it is clear that they gather without Him forcing them. Here in Joel 3:9-12a, Joel 2:2-10 is described again and God is calling on the might of the Gentile armies and challenging them to come up and do battle, and attack His people in the valley of Jehoshaphat.

(9) Proclaim this to the nations:	Proclaim this among the nations:
Let it be war!	Prepare for war!
Rouse up your warriors,	Rouse the warriors!
Muster your fighting men, march!	Let all the fighting men draw near and attack.
(10) Hammer your ploughshares into swords,	Beat your ploughshares into swords
your pruning-hooks into lances.	and your pruning hooks into spears.
Let your weaklings think them warriors	Let the weakling say,
Let your cowards think them heroes!	I am strong!
(11) Let the nations rouse themselves and march to Judgment valley.	Come quickly all you nations from every side, and assemble there.
(*Moffatt*)	(*NIV*)

What a challenge! Come! Come with everything and everybody! Come and attack! Come and attack Jerusalem! But then ... then ... when the people of Israel are on the very point of extinction they will learn that "If God be for us who can be against us?" (Romans 8:31).

> Bring down your warriors, O Lord!
> Let the nations be roused;
> Let them advance into the valley of Jehoshaphat,
> > for there will I sit
> > to judge all the nations on every side. (Joel 3:11,12 *NIV*)

"I will sit in judgment there, on all the nations round" is how *Moffatt* puts those last words. What will be God's judgment on those nations? How will it be executed? That which was threatened in Joel 3:3-8 is

Joel's Prophecy: Past and Future

now carried out and the figurative language of verse 13 does not hide the severity of the judgment.

In with the sickle! —	Swing the sickle,
the harvest is ripe!	for the harvest is ripe.
Come, tread the winepress,	Come, trample the grapes,
tread it, it is full:	for the winepress is full
the troughs are overflowing	and the vats overflow –
with their wickedness. (*Moffatt*)	so great is their wickedness! (*NIV*)

In Genesis 15:12-21 Abraham and his seed were promised a land which they could not immediately occupy because the iniquity of those who then possessed it was "not yet full" (Genesis 15:16, *KJV*). "For the sin of the Amorites has not yet reached its full measure" is how the *NIV* puts it. The Amorites had not become bad enough for God to step in and judge them, but when that Amorite cup was full ... then judgment came. The same is true of this future time that Joel is describing. When the cup of iniquity of the nations opposing Israel is full and overflowing, then God will step in and act. How large that cup is, one cannot say, but it becomes full during that great and terrible Day of the Lord, and Joel 3:13 implies that it is full to overflowing.

The parable of the tares in the field (Matthew 13:24-30) and its interpretation (Matthew 13:36-43) may be of some help here. The "reapers are the angels" (Matthew 13:39) and the time is "the end of the age" (Matthew 13:40; "age" is better than "world"). Thus the "mighty ones" of Joel 3:11 (*KJV*) are the angels who are told to "put ye in the sickle" (Joel 3:13). However, the Parable of the Tares seems to be dealing with the wicked within Israel, whereas in Joel it is the invading Gentile nations.

Joel 3:14-16: Multitudes, multitudes in the valley of decision! For the day of the LORD is near in the valley of decision. The sun and moon will be darkened, and the stars no longer shine. The LORD will roar from Zion and thunder from Jerusalem; the earth and the sky will tremble. But the LORD will be a refuge for his people, a stronghold for the people of Israel.

In Joel 3:14-16 there is repetition of some which has gone before. There are multitudes in the valley of decision (judgment) encamped around Jerusalem. Tension is high. The climax. of their battle is nigh. The sun, moon and stars are darkened and then ...

> The LORD will roar from Zion and thunder from Jerusalem; the earth and the sky will tremble. (Joel 3:16)

> On that day his feet will stand on the Mount of Olives, east of Jerusalem, and the Mount of Olives will be split in two from east to west, forming a great valley, with half of the mountain moving north and half moving south. (Zechariah 14:4)

No wonder Joel says "the earth and the sky will tremble". No wonder Joel says:

> The Lord will be a refuge for His people, a stronghold for the people of Israel. (Joel 3:16)

Just try and picture the situation. What will those armies think? There they are ... encamped about Jerusalem ... waiting for the final order to attack and annihilate the inhabitants ... that order comes ... they attack ... they advance ... they gain entry into the city ... into the Temple ... victory is ... and then ...

> The LORD will roar from Zion and thunder from Jerusalem; the earth and the sky will tremble. (Joel 3:16)

Can we paint an adequate picture of this incredible scene in our poor writings? Alas, no!

Joel 3:17-21: "Then you will know that I, the LORD your God, dwell in Zion, my holy hill. Jerusalem will be holy; never again will foreigners invade her. In that day the mountains will drip new wine, and the hills will flow with milk; all the ravines of Judah will run with water. A fountain will flow out of the LORD's house and will water the valley of acacias. But Egypt will be desolate, Edom

a desert waste, because of violence done to the people of Judah, in whose land they shed innocent blood. Judah will be inhabited forever and Jerusalem through all generations. Their bloodguilt, which I have not pardoned, I will pardon." The LORD dwells in Zion!

At the end of the longest section dealing with the removal of evil, Joel returns to the good which is to be bestowed. Verses 17 and 18 describe a peaceful, agricultural paradise and, here again, is the start of the Millennium. The Lord is dwelling in Zion, Jerusalem, and "never will foreigners invade her again" (*NIV*), which may better than "no strangers[7] pass through her any more" (*KJV*).

Waters and fountains in Joel 3:18 are also mentioned in Zechariah 14:8 but the passage which deals with this in much detail is Ezekiel 47:1-12. Joel 3:19 again mentions the removal of evil with references to Egypt and Edom, two past enemies of the people of Israel, and to the wrongs which they committed, but Joel's conclusion is ...

> "Judah will be inhabited for ever
> and Jerusalem through all generations
> Their blood guilt, which I have not pardoned,
> I will pardon." (Joel 3:21)

> "No longer will a man teach his neighbour,
> or a man his brother, saying, 'Know the LORD,'
> because they will all know me,
> from the least of them to the greatest,"
> declares the LORD.
> "For I will forgive their wickedness
> and will remember their sins no more."
> (Jeremiah 31:34)

---

[7] The Hebrew word *zanim* implies 'hostile' strangers (Jeremiah 51:51). However, there will be 'friendly' strangers and Gentiles in the restored kingdom (Isaiah 2:1-14; 61:5).

So Israel are forgiven and saved and become a Kingdom of Priests at last (Exodus 19:6). The kingdom of the Lord's Prayer is at last set up; His will is to be done on earth as it is done in heaven (Matthew 6:10). Nations will be at peace with one another and will go up to Jerusalem to learn the ways of the Lord (Isaiah 2:3-4). Why go to Jerusalem? Because …

The Lord dwells in Zion!
(Joel 3:21)

JEHOVAH SHAMMAH!

8. Joel and the Day of Pentecost

We now turn to one of the most well-known passages of the New Testament, Acts 2:1-21. It was on the day of the Jewish feast of Pentecost that the Holy Spirit descended upon those present and they spoke "with other tongues ... the wonderful works of God", (verses 4 and 11). There can be little doubt that this is one of the most misunderstood and misapplied passages of Scripture. In response to the question, "What does this mean?" Peter referred to Joel 2:28-32 (Acts 2:12,16-21). Ignorance of the original setting from which Peter quoted, and how the Jews of that time referred to their Prophets, have been contributory factors. Thus it was necessary for us to have first studied the whole of the book of Joel before turning our attention to Peter's speech on that great day. However, before a detailed consideration it may be an idea to look at one or two points about Old Testament prophecy in general.

In Isaiah 61:1-3 we read:

> The Spirit of the Sovereign LORD is on me, because the LORD has anointed me to preach good news to the poor. He has sent me to bind up the brokenhearted, to proclaim freedom for the captives and release from darkness for the prisoners, to proclaim the year of the LORD's favour and the day of vengeance of our God, to comfort all who mourn, and provide for those who grieve in Zion - to bestow on them a crown of beauty instead of ashes, the oil of gladness instead of mourning, and a garment of praise instead of a spirit of despair. They will be called oaks of righteousness, a planting of the LORD for the display of his splendour.

If we put ourselves back into the Old Testament times, blot out our knowledge of the New Testament, and try to ascertain how this prophecy would be accomplished, we will have problems. We might rejoice that "the *day* of vengeance" is shorter than the "the *year* of the Lord's favour" but ... well ... how can both come true at the same time? How can all that which is contained in these verses come about at one time?

Fortunately that is not our problem. We have a completed Bible and our problem is solved by our Saviour, Himself, in Luke 4:16-21. There the Lord Jesus Christ opened the book of the prophet Isaiah and began to read at the beginning of chapter 61. He started the chapter but read only as far as the first part of verse 2. This is what Luke records:

> The scroll of the prophet Isaiah was handed to him. Unrolling it, he found the place where it is written:
>
> "The Spirit of the Lord is on me, because he has anointed me to preach good news to the poor. He has sent me to proclaim freedom for the prisoners and recovery of sight for the blind, to release the oppressed, to proclaim the year of the Lord's favor."
>
> Then he rolled up the scroll, gave it back to the attendant and sat down. The eyes of everyone in the synagogue were fastened on him, and he began by saying to them, "Today this scripture is fulfilled in your hearing." (Luke 4:17-21, *NIV*)

The first verse and a half of Isaiah 61 were fulfilled at our Lord's first coming. The second half of verse 2, "the day of vengeance", will be fulfilled at His Second Coming and much of what we have studied in Joel relates to that time. Isaiah 61:1-3 is an example of a "two-half" prophecy. In such prophecies one half is fulfilled at one time and the other half is fulfilled at a different time. Is Joel 2:28-32 a "two-half" prophecy? Some would maintain that Joel 2:28-29 was fulfilled during the Acts period and that verses 30-32 were not. They await fulfilment in the days leading up to the Second Coming of Christ. Is this view correct?

A different type of prophecy is found in Isaiah 7:10-16 where King Ahaz is told:

Joel's Prophecy: Past and Future

"Therefore the Lord himself will give you a sign: The virgin will be with child and will give birth to a son, and will call him Immanuel. He will eat curds and honey when he knows enough to reject the wrong and choose the right. But before the boy knows enough to reject the wrong and choose the right, the land of the two kings you dread will be laid waste. (Isaiah 7:14-16)

The word translated virgin in Isaiah 7:14 is *almah*[8] and can be translated 'maiden' or 'young woman'. In Isaiah 7:14 we have *ha-almah,* 'the' maiden, that is some specific maiden known to Ahaz, and *The Companion Bible* suggests:

"Behold the maiden is pregnant and beareth a son . . ."

Ahaz is told that before this son shall know right and wrong the kingdom of Judah shall be relieved of the two kings who oppress it (Isaiah 7:1,16). This happened. A child was born in the court of Ahaz and the two kings were defeated by the Assyrians (Isaiah 8:4). Thus the prophecy of Isaiah 7:14-16 was accomplished within a short period of time.

That event, however, did not exhaust that prophecy which is taken up by the Holy Spirit in Matthew 1:23 and used of the miraculous birth of our Lord Jesus Christ. There the Greek word *parthenos,* which does mean virgin, was used of Mary.

The Holy Spirit took Isaiah 7 and used it in this very different way. This is an example of a "double" fulfilment of a prophecy. In such prophecies the first may be a partial fulfilment and the second a total one; or the first may be total but the second may result in something greater and grander.

Is Joel 2:28, 29 an example of a prophecy which is to have a "double" fulfilment? Some would maintain that the Acts period was only a partial fulfilment and that there is to be a future total fulfilment. Is that view correct?

---

[3] The *Septuagint* here has the Greek *parthenos*, as in Matthew 1:23. A word which unambiguously mean 'virgin'.

The latter rain

A common view held by some Pentecostals and Charismatics claims that their movements seen today are the fulfilment of the latter rain of Joel's prophecy. Their assertion is that Joel's prophecy of 2:28-29 has a double fulfilment because of the mention of former rain and latter rain in Joel 2:23 (see *KJV*: *NIV* has autumn and spring rains). They suggest the former rain was the fulfilment during the Acts period and the latter rain is the phenomena now seen in some parts of the world. Is this a valid interpretation of Joel 2:23,28-29?

From our study of Joel we have seen that the verse which deals with the former (autumn) and latter (spring) rain comes in the section dealing with temporal blessings bestowed upon the land of Judah, the animals and the people of Jerusalem and Judah; (Joel 2:21-27). The setting is very agricultural and, as we have seen, the former rain and the latter rain are just that! The rain is exactly what it says it is. It is literal rain. The former rain falls in October and November and the latter rain is to fall in March and April. Is it right to take part of a verse out of its true setting and context and "spiritualize" it as some have done? Is this rightly dividing the Word of Truth? Is this correctly handling the Word of God (2 Timothy 2:15)? We think not but ...

Let us assume that we are wrong on this point and that such an "interpretation" of the former rain and latter rain is valid. In that case we ask where is this latter rain to fall? The answer must be in the same place as the former rain — Jerusalem and the surrounding countryside. The whole idea of former and latter rain is applicable to that land only, and we cannot escape that fact. If there were to be such a latter rain fulfilment of Joel 2:28, 29 it would take place in Jerusalem and Judea, not elsewhere in the world. Some will wriggle and wrest the Scriptures (2 Peter 3:16) from their context and make this latter rain apply to anywhere in the world but this just cannot be. However ...

Let us assume that we can allow this "interpretation" of latter rain and allow it to fall anywhere and everywhere in the world. In that case we would ask 'when' is this latter rain to fall? The answer to this question

Joel's Prophecy: Past and Future

shows that such views are at great odds with the Bible. From our study of Joel 2:21-27 we have seen that all the events described there, including the restoration of the latter rain, take place *after* the northerner of Joel 2:20 has been destroyed, which takes place when Christ returns. Thus this latter rain is to come *after* the Lord's second coming.

However, from the Scriptures we see that the 'latter' rain is 'literal' rain which is to fall on the land of Palestine *after* the return of Christ. It is *not* a second outpouring of the Spirit anywhere in the world sometime before His Second Coming.

Joel's Prophecy

Returning to our deliberations as to whether or not Joel's prophecy is a 'two-half' prophecy or one subject to a "double" fulfilment; to help us in our search we should consult other parts of the Scripture. Joel 2:30-31 deals with "wonders in the heavens and in the earth, blood, and fire, and pillars of smoke. The sun shall be turned into darkness, and the moon into blood." If we consider other parts of the Scripture which contain references to these events and search the context, we will be able to see if there is any mention of the outpouring of the Spirit or of miracles similar to those of the Acts period. Initially we shall look to see if such an outpouring of the Spirit, and / or miracles from God, take place before the Lord's return. Those who hold such views may be justified from other Scriptures.

Matthew 24:29-30 has wonders and signs in heaven, and Matthew 24:7 has signs on the earth (famine, pestilence, earthquakes). However we search the whole chapter in vain looking for any outpouring of the Spirit and there is no mention of any miracles from God. We do, however, note the many references to "deceit" or "deceive" (verses 4, 5, 11 and 24). There are also references to *false* prophets and *false* Christs (verses 11 and 24) and these shall deceive by using "great signs and wonders". Thus the only miracles mentioned here prior to our Lord's return are miracles of deceit!

Mark 13 is very similar, dealing with the days leading up to Christ's return. Again there are signs in heaven and earth, false Christs and false prophets showing "signs and wonders to *seduce*" (Mark 13:22; *KJV*; 'deceive', *NIV*).

Luke 21 is different. There are signs in heaven (verses 25 and 27) and on the earth (verse 11) but there is no mention of miracles from God.

What about Revelation? This is the book that has many references to the phenomena we are considering. Revelation 6:12-13 has signs in heaven and earth but again we search the context in vain for any outpouring of the Spirit or for any Acts period miracle or for any evidential miracles from God. The same is true of Revelation 8:5,7-11. Also Revelation 11:13-19. Also Revelation 16:17-21. In fact in all passages which describe signs in heaven and earth there is mention neither of the outpouring of the Spirit nor of miracles from God in the days prior to the return of Christ. It is only Joel 2:28-32 which seems to link them but in actuality does not. The outpouring of the Spirit is "afterwards", that is 'after' the return of Christ. The signs in heaven are "before the great and terrible Day of the Lord", that is 'before' the return of Christ.

If we search Revelation we do find miracles in the days leading up to Christ's return, but they are not the working of God's Holy Spirit.

> Then I saw another beast, coming out of the earth. He had two horns like a lamb, but he spoke like a dragon. He exercised all the authority of the first beast on his behalf, and made the earth and its inhabitants worship the first beast, whose fatal wound had been healed. And he performed great and miraculous signs, even causing fire to come down from heaven to earth in full view of men. Because of the signs he was given power to do on behalf of the first beast, he deceived the inhabitants of the earth. He ordered them to set up an image in honour of the beast who was wounded by the sword and yet lived. (Revelation 13:11-14)

Here we see "deadly wound was healed" — the ability to raise the dead! "Fire from heaven" — the miracle God used with Elijah to prove His existence. Here we see Satan's beast, the false prophet, copying

Joel's Prophecy: Past and Future

God. Here Satan is pretending to be God and is causing deceit. Unless those miracles done in Satan's power are replicas of God's miracles recorded in Scripture, they will not have the desired effect. They will not *deceive* anyone. They must be copies and 2 Thessalonians 2:9-10 describes them as ...

> ... the work of Satan displayed in all kinds of counterfeit miracles, signs and wonders, and in every sort of evil that deceives those who are perishing.

The *KJV* has "signs and *lying* wonders, and with all deceivableness". These are strong words and people who dabble in miracles in days prior to Christ's return, and that includes these days in which we live, be warned ... Matthew 7:21-23 is salutary.

In 1 Timothy 4:1-3 we read of those who follow "deceiving spirits" ('seducing' spirit, *KJV*). 2 Timothy 3:8 states that "just as Jannes and Jambres withstood Moses, so also these men resist the truth".

Jannes and Jambres were the magicians of Pharaoh in Exodus 7:11 How did they withstand Moses? They copied the miracles that Moses performed (e.g. see Exodus 7:11,22; 8:7). Thus we cannot escape the fact that those who dabble with miracles in this age of full grace open themselves to the deceit of Satan. Some may ask, are there no evidential miracles of God promised for those days prior to Christ's return? There are but two.

Revelation 11:3-12 records that God is to miraculously support the two witnesses He shall have in Jerusalem for the 3 ½ years prior to His return. Revelation 12:6,14 and 16 records that God is to feed and protect the people of Israel in the wilderness during the same period. There are no other miracles recorded which relate to these times and note, these two miracles are centred at Jerusalem and the surrounding countryside. Thus we come to the conclusion that there is no second fulfilment of Joel's prophecy — neither at present in this dispensation nor in the days just prior to the Lord's return. Such a position cannot be justified from Scripture.

Some suggest that Joel's prophecy was totally fulfilled in the Acts period but that cannot be. Joel 2:28 has "And *afterwards* I will pour out my Spirit on *all* people." Even if we limit 'all people' to the people of Israel, as we have suggested, this did not happen in the years following Christ's ascension. Only some people enjoyed the benefits of the Spirit.

Also the "afterwards" in Joel 2:28 shows us that this pouring out of the Spirit is to be fulfilled 'after' many events — the most significant of which is the return of Christ. If this is the case we may well ask why did Peter quote from Joel on the day of Pentecost? How is Pentecost related to Joel's prophecy? What really happened on that day? First let us look at the events leading up to Acts 2.

Events leading up to Pentecost

The Lord Jesus Christ, Emmanuel, had been born. His death was for the world but His life was kept, in the main, to the people of Israel. He was their Prophet, Priest and King but ... they rejected Him ... they crucified Him. Scripture puts the responsibility for His death upon the shoulders of the Jewish people (Matthew 27:24, 25; Acts 5:30; 10:39). So was that the end of the people of Israel as God's chosen people? Was that the end of their hopes for their kingdom? No!

The ever gracious One, even as He was suffering, prayed "Father, forgive them, for they do not know what they are doing" (Luke 23:34). That was not a prayer for the Romans for they were not held responsible. That was a prayer for His earthly people and that prayer was obviously answered. They were not cut off at the Cross. After His resurrection He taught the disciples all things from the Scripture (Luke 24:44-48) and their first question was ...

> "Lord, are you at this time going to restore the kingdom to Israel?" (Acts 1:6)

The Acts period, the book of the Acts and the epistles written during it, contain information about the possible restoration of the kingdom to

Joel's Prophecy: Past and Future

Israel. To deny this, and to imply that the disciples "got it wrong" or "misunderstood", is a gross insult to the One who taught them. Would Israel be restored? They wanted to know but He declined to answer.

From what Peter preached in Acts 3:19-21 we see that the return of Christ, and thus the restoration of the kingdom to Israel, was dependent upon the repentance of the people of Israel.

> "Now, brothers, I know that you acted in ignorance, as did your leaders, but this is how God fulfilled what he had foretold through all the prophets, saying that his Christ would suffer.
> Repent, then, and turn to God,
> **so that** your sins may be wiped out,
> **[so] that** times of refreshing may come from the Lord, and
> **[so] that** he may send the Christ,
> who has been appointed for you - even Jesus. He must remain in heaven until the time comes for God to restore everything, as he promised long ago through his holy prophets." (Acts 3:17-21)

A call to repent was a feature of Joel (2:12-13) and his prophecy was also about the setting up of this kingdom. No doubt, in His post resurrection teaching the Lord had given Peter and company perfect understanding of this prophecy.

However, would this nation now respond to Peter's plea? Would they repent? Would Christ return? God in all His graciousness, having forgiven them the iniquity of crucifying Christ, leaned over backwards in an attempt to put things clearly before this people. Hebrews 6:5 describes that generation as those:

> ... who have tasted the goodness of the Word of God and the powers (Greek *dumanis* = miracles) of the coming age.

To those Acts period Jews, God had given a taste of "the powers (miracles) of the coming age". What is the "coming age" to which Hebrews refers? It can only be the kingdom to be set up when Christ returns, the Millennium kingdom. And the powers (miracles) must refer to the outpouring of the Spirit and the ensuing miracles. Thus God allowed the Jews of the Acts period a foretaste of the great blessings of the Millennium. He was imploring them, so to speak, to repent and accept Christ as their Messiah. Isaiah had shown that this Millennial kingdom age would be a time of great blessing "He who dies at a hundred will be thought a mere child" (Isaiah 65:20). Thus the raising of the dead during the Acts period would have had a special significance for the Jew. Those raised, if the nation repented, would see the return of Christ and live a much lengthened life in the kingdom, but note the last part of Isaiah 65:20.

> He who fails to reach a hundred will be considered accursed. (*NIV*)

> But the sinner being an hundred years old shall be accursed. (*KJV*)

Sadly Ananias and Sapphira had a foretaste of such a judgmental curse; Acts 5:1-11.

However, without going into greater detail we can appreciate that, for the Jew, the Acts period was a foretaste of the miracles or powers of the age which was to come, the kingdom age upon this earth, the Millennium. Thus the Acts period is not a 'fulfilment' of Joel's prophecy, but a 'foretaste' of it.

In the New Testament, when an Old Testament prophecy is fulfilled, it is common to read words such as "accomplished" or "as it is written ..." or "then it was fulfilled ..." but no such words are found in Acts 2. There Peter is *not* claiming that the events on the day of Pentecost are a 'fulfilment' of Joel 2:28, 29. This is not surprising. The main feature of the day of Pentecost was the gift of tongues, but this is not mentioned in Joel 2:28-29.

The gift of tongues, according to 1 Corinthians 14:21-22, was "a sign, not for believers but for unbelievers." Verse 21 is a reference back to Isaiah 28:11,12; 33:19 and Deuteronomy 28:49. To the Jews, the use of a tongue in an unknown language[9] was a sign to them of their unbelief. In Old Testament times it was unbelief in Jehovah and His Written Word, the Mosaic Law. Then they heard the tongues of foreigners, the unknown languages of the Assyrians and Babylonians. In the Acts period it was unbelief in Jehovah manifest in the flesh, Emmanuel, the Living Word of God, and they heard various unknown languages. As well as leaning over backwards by giving the Jews a foretaste of the foretold Millennial miracles, God added the miracle of tongues to indicate to them their unbelief and it provoked them to ask "What does this mean?" (Acts 2:12). Did this produce the desired effect?

Although some Jews did repent and believe in Jesus, the majority, and especially their leadership, did not, and so God allowed the Gentiles of the Acts period, to share in the miracles and blessings and hope of Israel. According to Romans 11:11-24 these Gentiles were like wild olive branches, grafted into the cultivated olive tree of Israel (verse 17). This was an attempt to provoke Israel to envy and emulation, (which is a better translation than 'jealousy' in the *KJV*, verse 11). Would the olive tree of Israel now bear fruit? Would they repent and believe in Jesus Christ? They had a foretaste of the Millennial miracles; they had the special gift of tongues to point out their unbelief; they had the stimulus of the wild olive; would Israel now repent of their unbelief and rejection of Christ?

Sadly — no! In Acts 28:17 Paul debated with the Jewish leaders but they failed to reach agreement. And Josephus tells us that at this time, the High Priest, Ananus, had James, the Lord's brother and leader of the Jerusalem church, and other leading Christians, stoned to death in Jerusalem. Acts 28:26-27 indicate the sad state of the nation of Israel. They had so hardened their heart against Christ that they were blind and deaf.

---

[9] For a thorough treatment of this see Michael Penny's *The Miracles of the Apostles* and the chapter on tongues: further details on page 107..

"'Go to this people and say, "You will be ever hearing but never understanding; you will be ever seeing but never perceiving."

For this people's heart has become calloused;
they hardly hear with their ears,
and they have closed their eyes.
Otherwise they might see with their eyes, hear with their ears, understand with their hearts and turn, and I would heal them."

This was the time when the nation of Israel was laid on one side by God and lost their privileged position as His chosen people. One day, they will be restored, as we have been seeing in Joel's prophecy. However, in Acts 28:28, God announced:

"Therefore I want you to know that God's salvation has been sent to the Gentiles, and they will listen!"

Gentiles were now to be blessed independently of the Jew. Individual Jews could still be saved, but now they were on a complete equality with Gentiles (Ephesians 3:6). From that point on Christians no longer looked for Christ to soon[10] return and set up the kingdom, and there is no mention of the possibility of Christ returning in the letters written after this time; see Ephesians, Philippians, Colossians, 1 & 2 Timothy, Titus, Philemon.

God revealed something new; His great plan for the heavenly places so magnificently described in the first three chapters of Ephesians. Christians could look forward to being in the heavenly places in Christ where, in coming ages, they would enjoy the incomparable riches of God's grace (Ephesians 2:6-8; note also Ephesians 1:3).

The evidential miracles, so closely linked with the people of Israel and the earthly kingdom, and so common during the period of time covered by the Acts of the Apostles, began to disappear. Paul had told the Corinthians that this would happen.

But where there are prophecies, they will cease; where there are tongues, they will be stilled; where there is [the gift of]

---

[10] For more on this see the next chapter.

Joel's Prophecy: Past and Future

knowledge, it will pass away. (1 Corinthians 13:8)

At the end of Acts is when this began to happen. In the books written after the end of Acts 28 there is no mention of such gifts as healing or tongues or knowledge, (see Ephesians, Philippians, Colossians, Philemon, 1 and 2 Timothy and Titus).

We read of many complete and instant healings not only performed by Christ in the Gospels, but also by the Apostles during Acts. However, we do not read of one in the letters written after Acts 28:28. Paul did not heal either Timothy (1 Timothy 5:23) or Trophimus (2 Timothy 4:20), and neither did he heal Epaphroditus, but thankfully he did recover (Philippians 2:26-27). This shows that the days of instant, complete, universal healing[11] were over. The evidential miracles from God ceased at the end of the Acts period and will not return until 'after' the return of the Lord Jesus Christ.

Any miracles which do appear in the years just prior to His Second Coming will be deceiving miracles, replicas of God's miracles, and the power behind them will ultimately be Satan's.

Conclusion

Drawing all ends together we can make the following deductions:

Joel 2:28-29 was not totally and completely fulfilled in the Acts period. During that time the Spirit was *not* poured out upon all Israel, but only upon some.

Also the context of the whole of Joel 2:21-29 is 'after' the northerner had been destroyed (verse 20) which takes place at the return of Christ. Therefore, total fulfilment of Joel could not have taken place in the Acts period.

---

[11] For more on the miracle of healing see Michael Penny's *The Miracles of the Apostles* and the chapter on healing: further details on page 107.

However, if the people of Israel had repented during the period of time covered by the Acts of the Apostles, then the Lord would have returned (Acts 3:19-21), the kingdom would have been set up, and the outpouring of the Spirit upon *all* people would have taken place. Pentecost could be described as a bud which could have blossomed into a full bloom — but sadly it didn't.

To say whether or not Joel 2:28, 29 is a prophecy that is subject to a 'double' fulfilment may involve one in the splitting of hairs.

Nowhere does Peter claim the Acts period or the day of Pentecost to be such. Nowhere is it said "then it was fulfilled ..." or "as it is written ..." or that it "is accomplished". Instead Peter says "this is that which was spoken by the prophet Joel".

However Hebrews 6:5 indicates that the Jews of the Acts period were given a foretaste of the Millennial miracles spoken of by Joel, and the gift of tongues, not mentioned by Joel, was added to indicate to them their unbelief and lack of faith[12]. Thus Pentecost and the Acts period is complicated but we would say that it was a 'foretaste'. However, a 'foretaste', however small, could be considered a partial fulfilment of Joel 2:28, 29. However, that passage waits for its total fulfilment, not in the days in which we live, neither in the days just prior to the Second Coming, but in the days following the return of our Lord Jesus Christ.

---

[12] See 1 Corinthians 14:22, and also the chapter on speaking in tongues in Michael Penny's *The Miracles of the Apostles* published by the Open Bible Trust: further details on page 107.

Joel's Prophecy: Past and Future

9. The Day of the Lord is at hand

One of the most difficult problems in Joel's prophecy is found in chapter 1 and verse 15:

> Alas for that day! For the day of the LORD is near; it will come like destruction from the Almighty. (*NIV*)

> Alas for the day! For the Day of the Lord is at hand and as a destruction from the Almighty shall it come. (*KJV*)

Well over 2000 years have passed and the Day of the Lord still has not come, yet Joel said it was 'near', it was 'at hand'. This nearness is again mentioned in Joel 2:1:

> ... for the day of the LORD is coming. It is close at hand. (*NIV*)

> ... for the Day of the Lord cometh, for it is nigh at hand. (*KJV*)

This problem will not go away. Joel 3:14:

> For the day of the LORD is near in the valley of decision.

How could Joel write that the Day of the Lord "is near", "is at hand", "is close at hand", "is nigh at hand", "is near"? This is indeed a problem and one which some commentators fail to face. We may not be able to fully understand what is meant here but prayerfully and in all humility we should consider it.

First this is *not* a problem of translation.

	Joel 1:15	Joel 2:1	Joel 3:14
KJV	is at hand	is night at hand	is near
RV	is at hand	is near	is near
RSV	is near	is near	is near
JND	is at hand	is at hand	is at hand
Moffatt	is near	near it is	is near
NEB	is near	is upon us	is at hand
NIV	is near	is close at hand	is near

"Is close at hand"! "Is upon us"! We search the book of Joel in vain for an answer but 1 Corinthians 2:13 exhorts us to compare "spiritual things with spiritual" (*KJV*). If we can find the same, or a similar, expression in Scripture and see how that is used, we may have a clue to help solve the problem in Joel.

Matthew 3 opens with John the Baptist preaching and in verse 2 we read that John said:

> "Repent, for the kingdom of heaven *is near*." (*NIV*)
> "Repent ye for the kingdom of heaven *is at hand*." (*KJV*)

He is not alone in this call. In Matthew 4:17 the Lord Jesus Christ started His ministry with the words ...

> "Repent, for the kingdom of heaven *is near*." (*NIV*)
> "Repent, for the kingdom of heaven is *at hand*." (*KJV*)

Mark 1:14,15 has similar words and if we understand that the kingdom referred to, and the repentance required, are the same as those referred to and required by the Old Testament prophets, then we can appreciate that we are again dealing with the repentance of Israel and the kingdom which is to come upon this earth. It is the kingdom of (from[13]) heaven; i.e. the

---

[13] In places like Matthew 3:2 and 4:17 where we read of "The kingdom of heaven" the 'of' is the Genitive of Origin (see *The Companion Bible*). It marks the source from which anything has its origins. For example 'visions of God' means visions proceeding from God; 'righteousness of

kingdom which originates in heaven, the kingdom from heaven which is to come upon this earth and which the Lord taught His disciples to pray for (Matthew 6:10). But although this kingdom was at hand, it wasn't set up. Instead of solving the problem of Joel we seem to have added to it. Let's add more! In Matthew 16:28 the Lord stated:

> "I tell you the truth, some who are standing here will not taste death before they see the Son of Man coming in his kingdom." (*NIV*)

> "Verily I say unto thee, there be some standing here which shall not taste of death, till they see the Son of man coming in *His* kingdom." (*KJV*)

This is repeated in Mark 9:1 and Luke 9:27. Some claim that this was fulfilled at the transfiguration which took place soon after (Matthew 17:1-9), but that does not seem to be correct especially as Mark 9:1 has:

> "I tell you the truth, some who are standing here will not taste death before they see the kingdom of God come *with power*." (*NIV*)

> "… shall not taste of death till they have seen the kingdom of God come *with power*." (*KJV*)

The transfiguration was a vision (Matthew 17:9; *KJV*). It was not the kingdom with power. Then in Matthew 24:34 and Luke 21:32 we read that Christ said to the disciples:

> "I tell you the truth, this generation will certainly not pass away until all these things have happened." (*NIV*)

> Verily I say unto you, this generation shall not pass away till all these things be fulfilled." (*KJV*)

---

faith' means righteousness coming through faith. Hence the 'kingdom of heaven' means the kingdom which originates in heaven, which comes from heaven.

But that generation did pass away and 'all these things' did not happen! There are explanations which state that these verses mean that all the events described in the context will take place within the lifetime of some future generation, but that is far from satisfying. That is not how the disciples would have understood Christ's words.

Matthew 10:23 provides a worse problem:

> "I tell you the truth, you will not finish going through the cities of Israel before the Son of Man comes." (*NIV*)

> "Ye shall not have gone over the cities of Israel till the Son of man be come." (*KJV*)

What? The Second Coming of Christ with power and great glory before they had gone over the cities of Israel? Well ... it never happened. All these, and more, are problem passages and the solution to the difficulty is found in such places[14]. In each of these verses there is the word 'until' or 'till' or 'before'. Each of these is a translation of the same two Greek words *eos an*. The notes in the margin of *The Companion Bible* on these verses make interesting reading and we quote some of them.

Matthew 16:28	till = the particle *an* with the subjunctive mood gives this a hypothetical force.
Mark 9:1	till = Greek *eos an*. The particle *an* makes this clause conditional: this condition being the *repentance of the nation of Israel at the call of* Peter. Acts 3:19-26. cp. 28:25, 26.
Matthew 24:34	till = here with the Greek *an* and the subjunctive mood, marking the uncertainty which was conditional on the repentance of the nation. till all be fulfilled

---

[14] These, and other passages, are dealt with in Michael Penny's *40 Problem Passages*, published by The Open Bible Trust.

Joel's Prophecy: Past and Future

Luke 21:32	= till (Greek *eos an*) all may possibly come to pass (not the same word as fulfilled in verse 24). Had the nation repented at Peter's call in Acts 2:38; 3:19-26 "all that the prophets had spoken" would have come to pass.
Matthew 10:23	till = see the four 10:23; 16:28; 23:39; 24:34.

This makes interesting and enlightening reading and shows that, although in the English these seem very definite statements, in the original Greek some doubt is cast on the timing of the event. For example, it could happen within a generation, but it may not; it depends, and what it depended upon was the repentance of Israel. If they repented Christ would return, and the kingdom would be set up (Acts 3:19-21).

There is further support for the above. On pages 143 and 144 of volume 20 of *The Berean Expositor* Charles H. Welch writes on these verses:

> There is in each of these verses an untranslatable particle *an,* the effect of which is to make the sentence contingent upon something expressed or implied. We can gather from other Scriptures, for example Acts 3:19-21, that the Second Coming of the Lord would not take place while Israel remained unrepentant ...

Matthew 16:27,28 refers to the same coming and kingdom. That coming would take place either within the lifetime of some who heard the words, or, failing that, would be deferred. This is implied by the article '*an*', "if". Israel did not repent, though granted nearly forty years in which to do so and fulfil the implication of the "if". They failed to do so, and when the patience of the long suffering God reached its limit, they were set aside, and the possibility of the Lord's return during the lifetime of any of His early disciples ceased to be practical truth.

A third testimony comes from Walter Bauer's *A Greek-English Lexicon of the New Testament and Other Early Christian Literature.*

Arndt and Gingrich translated and adapted the fourth revised and augmented edition which states:

> **an**: A particle peculiar to Greek, incapable of translation by a single English word; it denotes that the action of the verb is dependent on some circumstance or condition.

Some translations do attempt to translate this particle, attempting to show that what the Lord said was a possibility, rather than a certainty. *Young's Literal Translation* uses the word 'may' and the *Westcott and Hort Interlinear* uses 'might'. In the following quotations, the italics and bold italics are mine, and are not in the original.

Matthew 10:23

W&H	But whenever they persecute you in the city, be fleeing to a different one. For amen I am saying to you, you *might* not not complete the cities of Israel until the Son of Man *might* come.
Young's	And whenever they may persecute you in this city, flee to the other, for verily I say to you, ye *may* not have completed the cities of Israel till the Son of Man *may* come.

Matthew 16:28

W&H	Amen I am saying to you, some of the ones standing here *might* not not taste death until *likely* (Gr *an*) they *might* see the Son of Man coming in the Kingdom of Him
Young's	Verily I say to you, there are certain of those standing here who shall not taste of death till they *may* see the Son of Man coming in his reign

Matthew 24:34

W&H	Amen I am saying to you, this generation should not not *likely* (Gr. *an*) pass away until all these things should occur.
Young's	Verily I say to you, this generation may not pass away till all these *may* come to pass.

Mark 9:1

W&H	And He was saying to them, Amen I am saying to you that some of the ones having stood here should not not taste of death until *likely* (Gr. *an*) they *might* see the kingdom of God coming in power.
Young's	And he said to them, 'Verily I say to you, That there are certain of those standing here, who *may* not taste of death till they see the reign of God having come in power.'

Luke 9:27

W&H	Truthfully I am saying to you some of the ones who having stood here should not not taste death until *likely* (Gr. *an*) they should see the kingdom of God.
Young's	and I say to you, truly, there are certain of those here standing, who shall not taste of death till they *may* see the reign of God.'

Thus we have solved one great problem and, in so doing, have solved another. There are some who think that the disciples were wrong to expect the return of the Lord Jesus Christ in their lifetime. These think that the apostles misunderstood, but the Lord Himself taught them. Those who hold such a view of the Apostles' writings must be wrong and they are because they fail to believe that when Peter said …

"Repent ... that He may send the Christ"

he meant …

"Repent ... that He may send the Christ."

This is recorded in Acts 3:19-21 and Peter could not have been wrong. He had been taught by the Lord Jesus for over three years, and the resurrected Christ, before His ascension, also taught them and "opened their minds so that they could understand the Scriptures" (Luke 24:45) This whole section, Acts 3:19-26, is the foundation of the Acts period and to fail to grasp it and understand it will cause many problems in other passages of Scripture. For example:

Romans 13:12	The night is nearly over, the day is almost here.
1 Corinthians 7:29	The time is short.
Hebrews 10:37	For in just a very little while, He who is coming will come and will not delay.
James 5:8	Be patient and stand firm, because the Lord's coming is near.
1 Peter 4:7	The end of all things is near.
1 John 2:18	This is the last hour ... it is the last hour

And there are others. These all point to the fact that the return of the Lord Jesus Christ was possible then and there, and that the Apostles expected it. All that was required was for Israel to repent but that was not forthcoming. The nation was laid aside by God at Acts 28:25-28 and the epistles written after that time (Ephesians, Philippians, Colossians, Philemon, 1 and 2 Timothy and Titus) make no mention of Christ returning soon, or if it being the last days or the last hour. The hope of the people of Israel was, and still is, His *parousia* — His coming to the Mount of Olives.

Conclusion

The letters written during the time covered by the Acts of the Apostles state that "The day is almost here", "It is the last hour", "the end of all things is near", "the Lord's coming is near".

This may be why Peter changed:

> And *afterwards*, I will pour out my Spirit on all people. (Joel 2:28),

to:

> In *the last days*, God says, I will pour out my Spirit on all people. (Acts 2:17).

The fact that Peter changed Joel's prophecy is another indication that he did not view the events of that time as the fulfilment of Joel 2:28-29.

Joel's Prophecy: Past and Future

For Peter, and for those alive during the Acts period, these could so easily have been the last days. If Israel had accepted Jesus as the Son of God, their Christ (Messiah) and Saviour, they would have been, for He would have returned then. The Acts period epistles say "the Lord's coming is near" and *what draws near can withdraw.*

This is also the case with the pronouncement of John the Baptist and the Lord Jesus Christ in Matthew 3:1 and 4:17 that "the kingdom of heaven is near." Again what draws near can withdraw, and it was withdrawn for the kingdom of (from) heaven to come upon this earth is dependent upon the second coming of Christ They rejected Christ, they did not repent and so the kingdom did not come in (Matthew 21:42-44).

Returning to Joel, we see there a call to repent and turn to the Lord (Joel 2:12, 13). Also in Joel we are told that the Day of the Lord was at hand, it had drawn near. It seems that always, these two have been related. Did the people respond to Joel's message? Did they repent and turn to the Lord? If Joel was written during the last days of the kings of Judah then we know that they did not. They continued in their wicked ways and remained in their apostasy. The nation was exiled to Babylon and the Day of the Lord, which had drawn near ... withdrew. What would have happened if that people had repented ... well, using the expression correctly and reverently, only God knows!

Appendix 1:
The Last Days

There are some who insist that the expression "the last days", as used by Peter in Acts 2:17, must refer to the period of time just prior to the Lord's return. From this they conclude that because Peter said ...

> "In the last days," God said, "I will pour out my Spirit on all people" (Acts 2:17)

... that there will be an outpouring of God's Holy Spirit, with accompanying miracles, during that time. Earlier, we have shown that in the prophetic scriptures the only miracles spoken about in days leading up to Christ's return are satanic ones. However, does the expression "the last days" *always* refer to the years leading up to Christ's Second Advent?

There are other people who are concerned as to why Peter changed the "afterwards" of Joel 2:28 to "the last days" of Acts 2:17. If the "afterwards" refers to after the Lord's return, as it certainly does (Joel 2:20-28), why does Peter change it to "the last days", if that is a period of time just prior to the second coming?

Both of these queries can be answered by *a Biblical* study of every reference to the enigmatic expression "the last days". The Hebrew is *acharith ha-yamim* and it occurs some fourteen times in the Old Testament where it is translated by such phrases as "the last days" or "the latter days" in the *KJV*. However, in the *NIV* the expression is frequently translated "in days to come"; i.e. referring to sometime in the future which the context must determine.[15] For example, Jacob, in Genesis 49:1-

---

[15] For a full discussion of each occurrence of 'the last days' – *acharith ha-yamim* and *eschatos hemera* (Greek) - see Michael Penny's *The Last Days! When?* published by The Open Bible Trust.

28, used the expression to indicate various times in the future. The full list of occurrences is given on the next page and readers may care to consider the verses in their contexts by studying the passages surrounding them.

1.	Genesis 49:1	read 49:1-28
2.	Number 24:14	read 24:10-25
3.	Deuteronomy 4:30	read 4:25-30
4.	Deuteronomy 31:29	read 31:25-31
5.	Isaiah 2:2	read 2:1-5
6.	Jeremiah 23:20	read 23:16-22
7.	Jeremiah 30:24	read 30:18-24 & note 31:1
8.	Jeremiah 48:47	read 48:35-47 & note 48:1-47
9.	Jeremiah 49:39	read 49:34-39
10.	Ezekiel 38:16	read 38:14-16 & note chapters 38 & 39
11.	Daniel 2:28	read 2:26-35
12.	Daniel 10:14	read 10:21 & note chapter 11
13.	Hosea 3:5	read 3:1-5
14.	Micah 4:1	read 4:1-7

In Genesis 49:1-28 (the first occurrence), Jacob tells his sons what shall befall their posterity "in the last days" (*KJV*). A detailed consideration of this chapter, and its fulfilment, shows that some of the events concerned a time when the nation entered the promised land and the inheritance was portioned by lots; (e.g. verses 7,14 and 15. Compare with Joshua 19:1,9). Others had their fulfilment during the reigns of David and Solomon or at the division of the kingdom after Solomon's death; (e.g. verses 3 and 4, 19, 23. Compare with 1 Chron. 5:1-6, 26; 5:18 and 12:8; Amos 6:6). Still others looked forward to the Messiah, (e.g. v.10).

Numbers 24:10-25 seems to have the second coming of Christ in view in verse 17 whereas Deuteronomy 31:29 uses the expression to refer to some unspecified time in the future. A detailed study of all occurrences in the Pentateuch, together with their contexts, leads to the conclusion that "the last days" is not a phrase which refers exclusively to a period of time just prior to the return of the Lord Jesus Christ. It *may* refer to those days but it is more likely to refer to another time. The context determines what part of the future is under consideration.

Isaiah 2:1-5, Micah 4:1-7 and possibly Jeremiah 30:24 use the words to describe the days just *after* the Lord's second coming; that is, of the early years of the Millennium kingdom upon this earth. On the other hand, in Daniel 2:28, it refers to the great span of time from Nebuchadnezzar's day to when the stone cut without hands smashes the ten toes of the dream image and sets up a kingdom on earth which can never be destroyed (verses 34,44). Then, if Ezekiel 38:16 is parallel to Revelation 20:7-9, the expression is used of the end of the millennium — quite a different period of time. Gathering all these thoughts together, in the Old Testament "the last days" is used in a variety of ways, referring to various future periods of time. For example:

1. Of the time of entry into the promised land.
2. Of events during or just after the reigns of David and Solomon.
3. Of events surrounding our Lord's first coming.
4. Of events just *prior* to His second coming.
5. Of events just *after* His second coming.
6. Of events at the end of the Millennium.
7. Of the span of time from Nebuchadnezzar's day to the setting up of the Millennial Kingdom.
8. Of some unspecified future time.

This may explain why the *NIV* has translated the expression "in days to come", rather than using the traditional "the last days".

The Septuagint (*LXX*) translation of the Old Testament was the version commonly used in the first century A.D. as few Jews could read Hebrew. It translates *acharith ha-yamim* by expressions such as *eschatos hemera*. There are but five references in the New Testament to 'the last days'.

1. Acts	2:17	read	2:14-36.
2. 2 Timothy	3:1;	read	3:1-9.
3. Hebrews	1:2;	read	1:1-4.
4. James	5:3;	read	5:1-6.
5. 2 Peter	3:3;	read	3:1- 4.

Acts 2:17 is the first occurrence and any diligent seeker of truth should be asking to which period *of* time is Peter referring? Naturally he cannot be thinking of the time when the nation entered the promised land, nor can he have in mind the reigns of David and Solomon but is he using the expression "the last days" to relate to the time around Christ's first coming? Or to the days just prior to His second coming? Or to days just after His second coming? Or to days at the end of the Millennium? Or to the great gap from the Day of Pentecost to the time when that Millennial Kingdom will be set up? Or to some unspecified time in the future? A study of Peter's speech (Acts 2:14-36) does not reveal an answer but as this part of the speech was a quotation from another book of the Bible, it would be sensible to go to that other book and see what it says.

Acts 2:17-21 is a quotation from Joel 2:28-32, and Joel 2:20-28 shows that the prophet is referring to a time just after the northerner has been destroyed, which occurs at Christ's Second Advent. Joel also refers to a time after the blessing on the land has been restored and such a blessing is bestowed in the early days of the Millennium. Thus Joel 2:28, 29 is concerned with the early years of the Millennium, the years just after the Lord Jesus Christ has returned with power and great glory. This is what Isaiah and Micah, and possibly Jeremiah, refer to as "the last days" (*KJV*). When Peter replaced Joel's "afterwards" with "the last days" he was not altering what the prophet had said but was using a different expression which could mean the same thing. It is modern day movements which insist upon a narrow and limited meaning of the expression, ignoring the testimony of the whole of Scripture, which changes the sense of both Joel's and Peter's words. The "last days" is a Scriptural expression which refers to a future period of time, from the writer's standpoint, but as to which specific future period, only the context, or other *related* Scriptures, can make clear.

Appendix 2: This is that (Acts 2:16)

(Reproduced from Appendix 183 of *The Companion Bible*)

1. *"This is that which was spoken by the prophet Joel."*
There is nothing in the words to tell us what is "this" and what is "that". The word "this" is emphatic and the word "But", with which Peter's argument begins, sets what follows in contrast. This shows that the quotation was used to rebut the charge of drunkenness (v. 13).

So far from these signs and wonders being a proof that "these men" were drunken, "this", said the apostle, is "that" (same kind of thing) which Joel prophesied would take place "in the last days". Peter does not say these *were* the last days, but this (that follows) is what Joel says of those days. He does not say "then was fulfilled", nor "as it is written", but merely calls attention to what the prophet said of similar scenes yet future.

Therefore to understand what Peter really meant by "this is that", we must turn to the prophecy of Joel. And in order to understand that prophecy, we must see exactly what it is about.

       Is it about the Christian Dispensation?

or

       The Dispensation of judgment which is to follow it?

or

       Is it about the Jew and the Gentile?

or

       Is it about the church of God?

2. The Structure on p. 1224 [of *The Companion Bible*] gives the scope of Joel as a whole, while that on p. 1227 gives that of the last member B (p.

                        Joel's Prophecy: Past and Future

1224) in which occur the "signs" to which Peter points in connexion with "this is that". From this it will be seen that the prophecy of Joel links up with the last clause of the "song of Moses" in Deuteronomy 32:43 (see Revelation 15:3), which ends:

> "And (He) will be merciful unto His Land and to His people?"

So Joel 2:18 begins:

> "Then will Jehovah be jealous for His Land, and pity His people."

"THIS", therefore is "THAT". It is the subject-matter and remote context of Acts 2:16. It concerns Jehovah's Land and Jehovah's People, and has consequently nothing to do with the church of this Dispensation. Peter calls "the house of Israel" (v. 36) to the very repentance spoken of in the call to repentance of Joel (1:14-2:17; see *A*, Structure, p. 1224).

3. But the key to the correct understanding of Peter's quotation lies in the word "afterward" of Joel 2:28. The question is, after what? This we can learn only from Joel himself. Peter does not explain it, nor can we understand it from Peter's words alone.

The Structure (p. 1227 of *The Companion Bible*) shows us that the whole subject of 2:18-3:21 is, — evil removed from the Land and the People, and blessing bestowed on both; and these are set forth alternately. In 2:28,29 we have spiritual blessings connected with the temporal of the previous verses, introduced thus:

> "And it shall come to pass AFTERWARD, that I will pour out My spirit upon all flesh," &c.

After what? The answer is AFTER the temporal blessings of vv. 23-27. It is important to note that the temporal precede the spiritual blessings. The Holy Spirit was not poured out on all flesh at Pentecost: only on some of those present. None of the great signs in the heavens and on earth had been shown. No deliverance took place in Jerusalem: both Land and People were still under the Roman yoke.

4. Thus, from a careful study of the two passages, it will be seen that there is a wide divergence between the statements of apostle and prophet on the one hand, and the general belief of Christendom, which the majority hold so tenaciously, not to say acrimoniously, that "the church" was formed at Pentecost (see App. 181 and 186), on the other.

a) There can be no mistake about the meaning of Joel's word "afterward". It is not the simple Heb. word *'ahar* = after (cp. Genesis 5:4, &c.), but the compound *'aharey-ken* = after that (as Genesis 6:4, &c.).

b) It is therefore certain that the word "this" in Acts 2:16 refers to what follows, and not to what precedes; to the future events predicted by Joel, and not to those then taking place in Jerusalem.

c) As Joel speaks of no gift of tongues, "this" cannot refer to these Pentecostal tongues, the outstanding cause of all the wonder and excitement.

d) None of the things detailed in vv. 17, 19 came to pass. "This" therefore could not be the fulfilment of Joel's prediction, as the "pouring out" was only on the apostles and those associated with them.

5. To sum up: As we have seen, there is in Acts 2:16 no fulfilment of Joel's prophecy either expressed or implied, and Peter's argument narrows down to this, viz. that a charge of drunkenness can no more be sustained against "these" than it can be against those in the yet future scenes spoken of by Joel, when the wondrous spiritual blessings will be poured out on all flesh AFTER THAT, i.e. after all the *temporal* blessings spoken of have been bestowed upon Israel's Land and Israel's People.

Joel's Prophecy: Past and Future

Appendix: Books quoted or referred to.

40 Problem Passages: Michael Penny

A Greek English Lexicon of the New Testament and other Early Christian Literature: Walter Bauer

Approaching the Bible: Michael Penny

Biblical Chronology: Peter John-Charles

Deuteronomy 28: A Key to Understanding: Michael Penny

Literal Translation of the Bible: Robert Young

Greek / English Interlinear New Testament: Westcott and Hort

The Believer's Guide to Bible Chronology: Charles Ozanne

The Berean Expositor

The Companion Bible

The Day of the Locust by Charles Ozanne

The Day of the Lord! When? By Michael Penny

The first printed English Bible: Miles Coverdale

The Last Days! When?: Michael Penny

The Miracles of the Apostles: Michael Penny

About the author

Michael Penny was born in Ebbw Vale, Gwent, Wales in 1943. He read Mathematics at the University of Reading, before teaching for twelve years and becoming the Director of Mathematics and Business Studies at Queen Mary's College Basingstoke in Hampshire, England. In 1978 he entered Christian publishing, and in 1984 became the administrator of the Open Bible Trust.

He held this position for seven years, before moving to the USA and becoming pastor of Grace Church in New Berlin, Wisconsin. He returned to Britain in 1999, and is at present the Administrator and Editor of The Open Bible Trust. In 2010 he was elected Chairman of Churches Together in Reading, where he speaks in a number of churches. He is one of the chaplains at Reading College and is on the Advisory Committee of Reading University Christian Union.

He lives near Reading with his wife and has appeared on BBC Radio Berkshire and Premier Christian Radio many times. He has made several speaking tours of America, Canada, Australia, New Zealand and the Netherlands, as well as ones to South Africa and the Philippines. Some of his writings have been translated into German and Russian.

He has written many major books including:
Paul: A missionary of Genius
Peter: His life and letters
Galatians: Interpretation and Application
Following Philippians (written with W M Henry)

For a full list of books written by Michael Penny please visit:

wwww.obt.org.uk/michael-penny

Michael Penny is editor of *Search* magazine

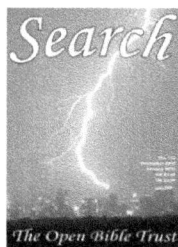

More on the Prophets

The Day of the Locust:
Joel and the Day of the Lord
Charles Ozanne

The book of Joel is about two days, two events. The first is The Day of the Locust: a locust infestation of unprecedented severity, but this was only the prelude to something far, far worse: The Day of the Lord. The challenge in understanding Joel is to distinguish between these two occasions. In his day the former had already happened, but the latter loomed on the horizon and could still be averted. Was it?

Charles Ozanne has written a number of books on the Minor Prophets.

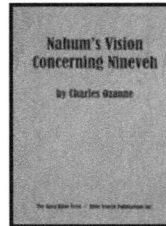

Hosea: Prophet to Israel – The Northern Kingdom
Nahum's Vision Concerning Nineveh
Malachi: The Lord's Messenger
The Book of Immanuel (Isaiah 7-12)
Amos: The Lion has roared

Further details on www.obt.org.uk
Copies can be ordered from www.obt.org.uk
They are also available as eBooks from Amazon and Apple
and as KDP paperbacks from Amazon.

Joel's Prophecy: Past and Future

Also by Michael Penny

The Miracles of the Apostles

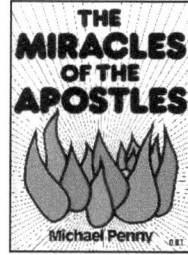

he Acts of the Apostles covers one of the most dramatic stages in God's plan for the people of Israel. They had rejected their Messiah with cries of "Crucify Him! Crucify Him!", but He had prayed "Father, forgive them, for they do not know what they are doing." That prayer was answered because it was through ignorance that both the common people and their leaders turned their backs upon Jesus and, under the Mosaic Law, a person who sinned through ignorance, or unintentionally, could be forgiven.

That being the case, the burning issue for the apostles was to ask the Lord, "Are you at this time going to restore the kingdom to Israel?" but they were not given a direct answer. They were told that "It is not for you to know the times or date the Father has set by his own authority" (Acts 1:6-7). Whether or not that kingdom would be restored to Israel at that time depended upon the response of that nation itself. It would be restored only when the King returned and set up His kingdom. Would He return soon? Would He come back within the lifetime of the apostles? That was the issue and, that, according to Peter, depended upon Israel repenting (Acts 3:19-21).

In order to encourage Israel to repent, and to ensure that they were without excuse if they failed to do so, the apostles were given the power to perform various wonders and signs. These were *The Miracles of the Apostles* and included speaking and interpreting tongues, knowledge and wisdom, healing and judgement, visions and voices, visitation and revelations, wonders in heaven above and signs on the earth beneath. All these and more, are considered in this book, which explains the significance and meaning these miracles should have had to the people of Israel.

"Miracles" were also "signs", a fact missed by the Gentiles of New Testament times, and missed by many Christians today.

**This book explains the significance of
each and every type of miracle
performed by the Apostles.**

Copies can be ordered from www.obt.org.uk

**It is also available as an eBook from Amazon and Apple
and a KDP paperback from Amazon.**

Publications of The Open Bible Trust must be in accordance with its evangelical, fundamental and dispensational basis. However, beyond this minimum, writers are free to express whatever beliefs they may have as their own understanding, provided that the aim in so doing is to further the object of The Open Bible Trust. A copy of the doctrinal basis is available at

www.obt.org.uk/doctrinal-basis

or from:

THE OPEN BIBLE TRUST
Fordland Mount, Upper Basildon,
Reading, RG8 8LU, UK.

www.ingramcontent.com/pod-product-compliance
Lightning Source LLC
Chambersburg PA
CBHW071454070426
42452CB00039B/1354